APM Guide to Contracts and Procurement

APM Guide to Contracts and Procurement: For Project, Programme and Portfolio Managers

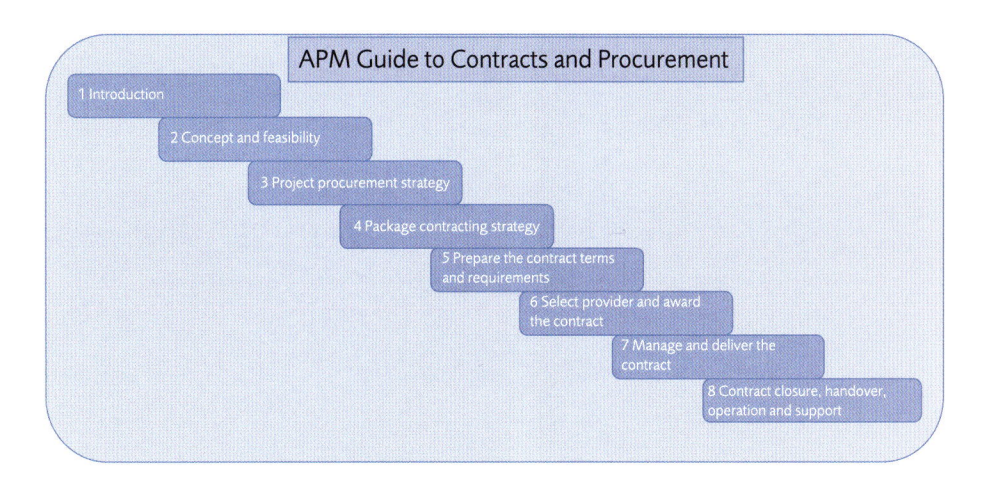

APM Guide to Contracts and Procurement

1 Introduction
2 Concept and feasibility
3 Project procurement strategy
4 Package contracting strategy
5 Prepare the contract terms and requirements
6 Select provider and award the contract
7 Manage and deliver the contract
8 Contract closure, handover, operation and support

Association for Project Management

Association for Project Management
Ibis House, Regent Park
Summerleys Road, Princes Risborough
Buckinghamshire
HP27 9LE

© Association for Project Management 2017

All rights reserved. No part of this publication may be reproduced, stored in a retrieval system, or transmitted, in any form or by any means, without the express permission in writing of the Association for Project Management. Within the UK exceptions are allowed in respect of any fair dealing for the purposes of research or private study, or criticism or review, as permitted under the Copyright, Designs and Patents Act, 1988, or in the case of reprographic reproduction in accordance with the terms of the licences issued by the Copyright Licensing Agency. Enquiries concerning reproduction outside these terms and in other countries should be sent to the Rights Department, Association for Project Management at the address above.

British Library Cataloguing in Publication Data is available.
Paperback ISBN: 978-1-903494-66-0
eISBN: 978-1-903494-67-7

Cover design by Fountainhead Creative Consultants
Typeset by RefineCatch Limited, Bungay, Suffolk
in 10/14pt Foundry Sans

Contents

List of figures and tables — vii
Preface — ix
Acknowledgements — x

1 Introduction — 1
   1.0 Who is this guide written for? — 1
   1.1 Background to this guide — 2
   1.2 How to use this guide — 11
   1.3 Key term definitions used in this guide — 12

2 Concept and feasibility — 15
   2.0 Overview — 15
   2.1 Background — 16
   2.2 Inputs — 17
   2.3 Activities — 17
   2.4 Outputs — 30

3 Project procurement strategy — 33
   3.0 Overview — 33
   3.1 Background — 34
   3.2 Inputs — 37
   3.3 Activities — 37
   3.4 Outputs — 52

4 Package contracting strategy — 53
   4.0 Overview — 53
   4.1 Background — 54
   4.2 Risk management — 54
   4.3 Inputs — 58
   4.4 Activities — 58
   4.5 Outputs — 88

5 Prepare the contract terms and requirements — 91
   5.0 Overview — 91
   5.1 Background — 92
   5.2 Inputs — 94

Contents

	5.3	Activities	100
	5.4	Outputs	111
6	**Select provider and award the contract**		**113**
	6.0	Overview	113
	6.1	Background	114
	6.2	Risk management	120
	6.3	Inputs	121
	6.4	Activities	123
	6.5	Outputs	140
7	**Manage and deliver the contract**		**141**
	7.0	Overview	141
	7.1	Background	142
	7.2	Inputs	142
	7.3	Activities	143
	7.4	Outputs	158
8	**Contract closure, handover, operation and support**		**161**
	8.0	Overview	161
	8.1	Background	162
	8.2	Inputs	164
	8.3	Activities	164
	8.4	Activity 1: Assign resources	165
	8.5	Activity 2: Contract closure	166
	8.6	Activity 3: Handover	169
	8.7	Activity 4: Ongoing operation, maintenance and support activities	170
	8.8	Outputs	172

Acronyms and abbreviations	**173**
Bibliography	**175**
Appendix A	**177**
Appendix B	**185**
Appendix C	**189**
Index	**193**

Figures and tables

Figures

1.1	The procurement guide life cycle stages	3
1.2	The requirements hierarchy expressed in a works contract	5
1.3	Expansion of the project life cycle (from *APM Body of Knowledge* 6th edition)	6
1.4	Cost influence curve (after Rocque)	9
1.5	The 'agile' values	10
2.1	Process diagram for the concept and feasibility stage	18
2.2	SWOT matrix	24
3.1	The requirements hierarchy expressed in a works contract	36
3.2	Process diagram for the project procurement strategy stage	37
3.3	Example package breakdown structure (PaBS)	45
3.4	PaBS development for a wind-farm project	45
3.5	The 'hard' and 'soft' boundaries for goods and services	46
3.6	Kraljic matrix (Kraljic 1983)	48
3.7	Buyer–supplier relationships (after Bensaou)	50
3.8	Correlating the nature of relationship with the project complexity and duration	51
4.1	Process diagram for the package contract strategy stage	59
4.2	Most appropriate collaboration strategy against contract complexity/timescale	64
4.3	A target cost contract with approximately 50:50 share of any over and under run compared with the target prices	71
4.4	Illustrating that the employer's share of any overrun is capped at approximately 10 per cent overrun on the target prices	71
4.5	Example contractual structure of a PFI arrangement	76
5.1	Process diagram for the prepare contract terms and requirements stage	101
6.1	Process diagram for the provider selection stage	123
6.2	Example value tree for a housing association appointment	126
7.1	Solution delivery phases	143
7.2	Manage and deliver the contract process	144

Figures and tables

7.3	Initiation stages	145
7.4	Deming circle	151
7.5	The change control process	154
7.6	Contract closure decision	157
8.1	Contract closure, handover, operation and support process	165

Tables

3.1	Example high-level package terms for a solar power station	38
3.2	Example 'make' or 'buy' criteria	41
6.1	Characteristics of differing procurement methodologies	127
6.2	Example scoring criteria	132
6.3	Example provider selection scoring table	136
A1	Typical risks associated with external contracting	178
C1	Red flags	189

Preface

Procurement and contract management is an increasingly important aspect to delivering successful projects, programmes and portfolios (P3), therefore an effective P3 manager must have a good understanding of procurement and contracting in order to manage these aspects. The APM's Contract and Procurement SIG offers this guide as a 'place to go' for P3 managers at all levels, so that they understand 'how to' procure works and manage delivery through the phases of the procurement life cycle.

Acknowledgements

Because of the length of time that it has taken to write this guide, many people have reviewed and made constructive suggestions over the years to the various drafts of this guide as it evolved. All of them receive our – the APM Contracts and Procurement SIG's – thanks.

As the original author of the early chapters of this guide and 'executive' editor, I would like to thank the following people who have co-authored chapters:

- Helen Barrow
- Anne Dwyer
- Steve Emerton
- Alastair Greenan
- John Lake
- Philip Reese
- Rob Soames

In addition, I give John Lake a special mention as, in consultation with others, he did the hard work in editing the later chapters into a common format. He then did most of the final editing of the whole guide as we approached publication. Without his efforts – and that of the others – it would still be 75 per cent complete. As such, John is very definitely the co-editor.

Dr Jon Broome BEng PhD MAPM
Co-editor and chair of the APM Contracts and Procurement SIG

1

Introduction

1.0 Who is this guide written for?

The intended audience for this guide is:

1. Project, programme and portfolio (P3) managers and project procurement professionals who require an easy to use 'how to' guide for procuring externally sourced 'works'.[1]
2. Stakeholders within organisations who wish to increase their awareness of how works can be procured e.g. financial officers, operational professionals, engineers, etc.

This guide is **not** aimed at those procuring standard off-the-shelf manufactured goods or standard consultancy services. There is already a wealth of good information available from other sources covering this type of procurement.[2]

The guide is applicable for those involved in both public and private sectors including those projects that are subject to European Union (EU) procurement rules.[3]

---

[1] The word 'Works' is the term used in EU Procurement for a procurement of a project or programme, as opposed to the purchase of goods and services (European Union, 1993). At the time of publication of this guide, the United Kingdom had voted to exit the European Union ('Brexit'). Despite this event, it is important to note that the prevailing EU Procurement Directives remain enshrined in law in the UK through Acts of Parliament. Consequently, even after Brexit the relevant EU legislation will still apply unless and until changed by an Act of Parliament.

[2] For free material and some you have to pay for go to the Chartered Institute of Procurement and Supply's (CIPS) website at www.cips.org (Chartered Institute of Procurement and Supply, n.d.) and click on resources. Alternatively, a book especially for project managers on this topic is by Ward, G. (2008) *The Project Manager's Guide to Purchasing – Contracting for Goods and Services*.

[3] We, however, point out that this guide should not be taken as definitive from a legal perspective and legal advice should always be taken on the respective legal matters. See also note 1 above.

1.1 Background to this guide

1.1.1 Managing procurement in a project context

Procurement covers a wide breadth of activities which may range from buying paper clips to contracting a new IT system, or the building of a new shopping centre. It is a common perception, however, that procurement should be handled by a specific purchasing resource or department rather than being a central competency within P3 management.[4] In complex projects this can – and we find frequently does – lead to unforeseen issues developing, leading to time cost and quality overruns due to the project manager being unaware of the pitfalls that can arise when contracting to third parties.

In this guide, we focus on the procurement of works in the form of 'packages'. These will typically have a higher level of uncertainty associated with them compared with the procurement of basic goods and services (commodities) and may form a substantial part of the main project. Indeed, the cost of such contracted-out packages may outweigh all other project spend. For example, each of the following packages may account for over 90 per cent of the total project spend:

- A contract for construction of physical asset.
- A contract to develop, install and manage an information technology capability.
- A contract for the supply of complex machinery designed and manufactured specifically for an employer.

The guide is based on the procurement life cycle stages as illustrated in Figure 1.1.

Chapter 1 of this guide provides an introduction, with follow-on chapters (2–8) addressing each life cycle stage. Chapters 2–8 are structured to enable the reader to quickly gain the necessary guidance relevant to each stage in the procurement life cycle to include:

- **Overview:** Defining the chapter content to enable the reader to understand whether the chapter addresses their immediate concerns

---

[4] P3: Project, programme and portfolio. We use the term 'project manager' in this guide to cover any P3 (project, programme and portfolio) management role.

Introduction

- **Background:** Providing further background for optional reading.
- **Inputs:** Listing what is needed at the stage start.
- **Activities:** Tasks to be performed based on the stage process diagram included.
- **Outputs:** What the stage provides when completed.

Where applicable, an additional section summarises the risk aspects that should be considered during the stage.

It should be noted that we define some specific terms which relate directly to contracts and procurement (e.g. the provider, the employer). Summary definitions of these terms are given in section 1.3 below. The guide also includes the generic definitions from the APM's *Body of Knowledge* series 6th edition and other prior learnt material, where applicable, in text boxes to assist the reader and provide a route to further research.

In this guide, we describe a generic process which can be followed regardless of the size of the project or programme. For a small procurement, it may mainly be a thought process. However, the larger the project or programme, the more thought should be applied with more formality in terms of recording the decisions made and reasons why. Indeed, for a major procurement exercise, this guide could be used as the starting point for the process of developing the required contracts and an aid to seeking further detailed advice or guidance if required.

We believe that you will find the following chapters a useful introduction to each of these activities and it will spur you on to further develop your understanding and skills in these areas.

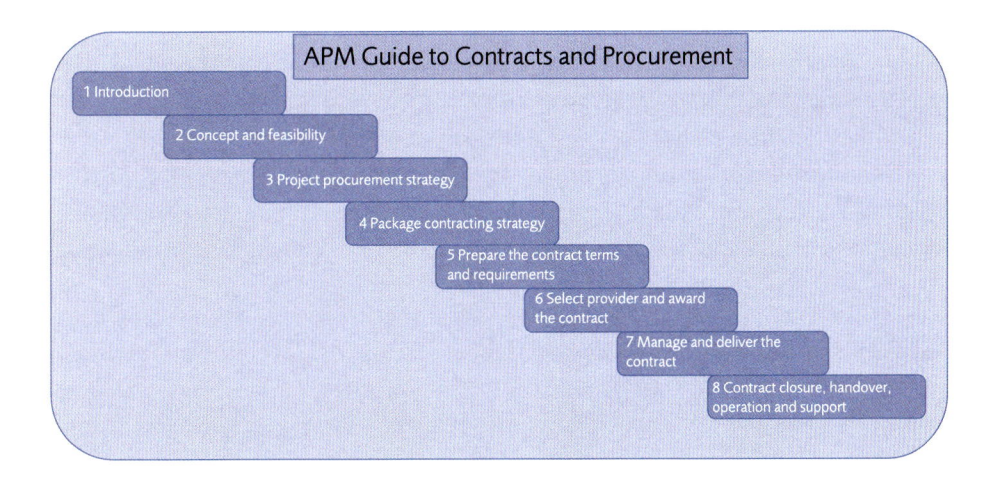

APM Guide to Contracts and Procurement
1 Introduction
2 Concept and feasibility
3 Project procurement strategy
4 Package contracting strategy
5 Prepare the contract terms and requirements
6 Select provider and award the contract
7 Manage and deliver the contract
8 Contract closure, handover, operation and support

Figure 1.1 The procurement guide life cycle stages

We stress that this is a *guide* to procurement within projects and is not 'the gospel'. In all likelihood, it will not be an absolute fit with how your organisation procures a project or for your particular project, so think of it as a starting point and for adaptation to fit.[5]

Additionally, below in this section we provide further background to support the development of the requirement and give some insight into the recent trends in outsourced package procurement, which is in constant development.

1.1.2 Developing the requirement

One approach might be, for example, when procuring a new building, to try to define or specify all the individual component parts of it. However, the sheer technical complexity of many unique project-based purchases means that it is almost impossible to specify every 'nut and bolt'. Nor is it usually appropriate, as the technical expertise to do so does not reside within the employer organisation. As a result, requirements are now commonly expressed in a contract as 'performance' or 'functional' specifications. For example, a performance specification might be for the data throughput and content that an IT system has to be able to handle, expressed in measurable units, leaving the selection of the specific individual goods and services to deliver these requirements to the provider. The provider may in-turn rely on the expertise of the specialist parties they subcontract with in their own supply chain.

The performance or functional requirements lead to contracts expressing the end capabilities or outputs that the employer wants from the project rather than the individual elements that make up the works.[6] For instance, combining an IT system with a help desk service provides a customer service capability. This capability may be expressed in measurable units of response time and customer satisfaction metrics, etc.

The supplied new or enhanced capabilities should lead to new or improved outcomes or benefits which align with the sponsoring employer organisation's mission and business objectives. In order for them to be meaningful, the outcomes

---

[5] Some example publications that can provide further background to contract management are: IACCM (2013) *Fundamentals of Contract and Commercial Management*; IACCM (2011) *The Operational Guide – Contract and Commercial Management*; and Nijssen, J. (2015) *When Contract Management Meets PRINCE2*.

[6] Note that in our experience, there is a grey line between what is a performance or functional specification and what is a capability or output specification.

Introduction

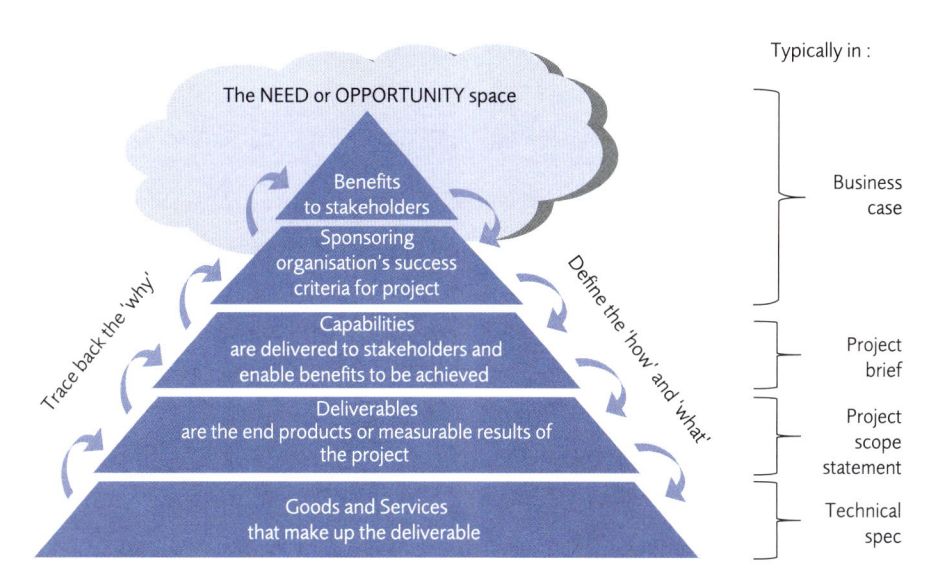

Figure 1.2 The requirements hierarchy expressed in a works contract

or benefits need to be expressed in objective and measurable terms, i.e. success criteria, which can be incorporated into a contract as deliverables against which the provider may be paid. Indeed, it may be the best contractual arrangement to make it conditional that the provider is paid on the basis of business outcomes or benefits delivered if they can be isolated to be sufficiently in the provider's control.

Figure 1.2 illustrates a hierarchy of detail reflecting how requirements can be expressed in a works contract.

1.1.3 Procurement trends

Trends in procurement over recent times have included:

- The expansion of the project life cycle to include all activities 'from cradle to grave' including operation and termination/disposal (see Figure 1.3). Rather than simply thinking of benefits in the operation phase, organisations are increasingly thinking and specifying requirements in terms of whole life benefits and costs, which is to say the inclusion of how the asset will be used and impact the core business.
- A contracting strategy where the provider is paid on the basis of capabilities or even benefits delivered in the operation phase is the 'design, build, finance,

APM Guide to Contracts and Procurement

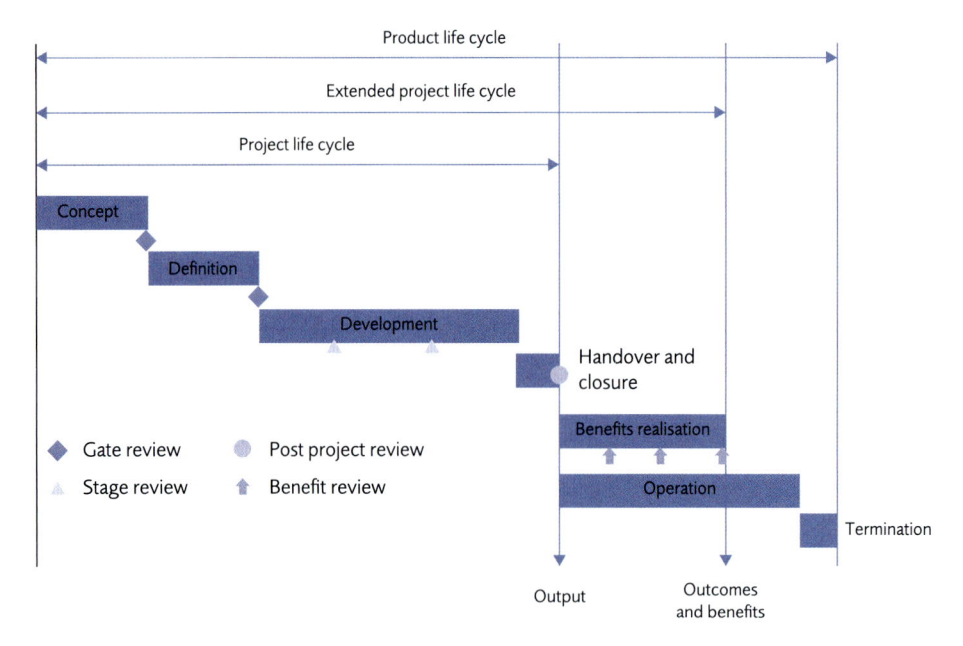

Figure 1.3 Expansion of the project life cycle (from *APM Body of Knowledge* 6th edition)

operate' concept; more commonly known as the private finance initiative (PFI) or public private partnership (PPP).
- An increasing need for collaboration in order to deliver projects, as no longer can a single organisation do it all due to the increasing complexity of both technology and society, in some sectors.
- Selection of providers, in some cases almost wholly, on the basis of their cultural and technical capabilities. This is increasing due to the 'end product' being not fully defined or being a moving target. What is being bought is therefore the capability to develop a solution rather than delivery to fixed start and end points. The procurement cycle is therefore increasingly used to leverage the know-how of the supply chain to deliver competitive advantage.
- Conditions of contract are being designed to align motivations and be more relationship based, i.e. define how parties work together, as opposed to trying and often failing to define illusory fixed end states. An example of this trend is the growing use of the New Engineering Contract version 3 (NEC3) family of contracts in the engineering and construction industries and elsewhere.
- The emergence of programme management; defined as:

Introduction

> **Programme management:** The coordinated management of projects and change management to achieve beneficial change. *APM Body of Knowledge 6th edition*

- A related development is the inclusion of portfolio management to create the 'P3' (Project, programme and portfolio) coverage in related texts.

> **Portfolio management:** The selection, prioritisation and control of an organisation's projects and programmes in line with its strategic objectives and capacity to deliver. *APM Body of Knowledge 6th edition*

For the rest of this guide we generally use the term 'project', unless the context dictates otherwise.

All of the above developments apply to work package procurement that supports projects and programmes of work, more so than to the purchase of manufactured goods and standard services. The general definition of procurement is given in the *APM Body of Knowledge 6th edition* (see below).

> **Procurement:** Procurement is the process by which products and services are acquired from an external provider for incorporation into the project, programme or portfolio. *APM Body of Knowledge 6th edition*

When we consider the way that procurement is developing today, its growing importance and its increasing complexity, this definition may need to evolve to cover the wider scope; where significant and pivotal packages are contracted to providers.[7] We have provided our updated definition for the purposes of this guide in section 1.3 below.

---

[7] Indeed, as the Greeks were carrying out procurements for projects and using contracts with many of the features associated with those used today, then there is a good argument for saying the APM definition is some 2400+ years out of date. See Soames, B. (2011), *Buying Just Like The Ancient Greeks: What Ancient Greek Purchasing Can Teach Us About Procurement Now*, Buy Research Publications.

APM Guide to Contracts and Procurement

For significant 'packages',[8] the employer needs to contract with providers that can be relied upon to deliver to the time, cost and performance parameters set out in the contract. Projects, being subject to risk and change, rarely run completely as planned at the outset. It is therefore imperative that both employer and provider organisations anticipate risk and change (and that the contract between them allows for it). Consequently, the competencies the employer's P3 manager[9] and the selected provider's project manager, as well as the quality of contract put in place between these organisations, will largely determine the success of the procured package and hence of the overall project.

Of course, poor contract management and administration can undermine good work done earlier in the procurement process. Conversely, it is also the case that the decisions made and actions taken at early points in the procurement process may substantially affect overall success or failure. Yet we find that it is often the case that an employer organisation may underestimate the required rigour needed at the early stages in the procurement cycle; for example, causing the selection of an inappropriate provider. This can lead to defensive positions being taken by either or both the employer and the provider should the delivery of the solution be subject to fall-offs in the expected time, cost and quality. This may ultimately become an unrecoverable situation with resulting impacts on time, cost and quality for either or both parties.

The key activities in the procurement process which we consider essential are described in this guide including:

- determining the procurement and contracting strategies for the project;
- preparing the contract terms;
- selection of the provider(s); and
- managing and delivering the contract and ultimately its closure.

The guide also covers the major influences and risks that can affect the outcome during delivery, including interaction with companion packages, as well as by the

---

[8] We use the term 'package' to reflect that an individual contract can be for a substantial part of a project and could be regarded as a project in itself, e.g. 90 per cent of the spend on a construction project could be on the contract to design and construct the asset.

[9] We use the term 'project manager' in this guide to cover any P3 (project, programme and portfolio) management role.

Introduction

> **The cost influence curve:** Prior study[10] has pointed out that it is early in the project that the ability to influence the outcome in terms of cost is the greatest. Typically, during the initial weeks/months of the project, the project's critical elements are shaped, including the involvement patterns of the project sponsor.
>
> **Figure 1.4** Cost influence curve (after Rocque)
>
> Conversely the investment in the project (its cost) rises throughout the project thus the risk of there being wasted investment also increases (for example if a provider needs to be changed due to performance or other issues developing).

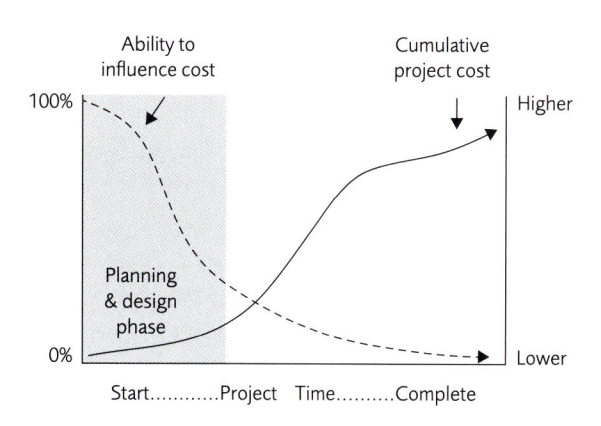

prevailing environment external to the project, e.g. changes in legislation, business context, politics, etc. The conditions of contract put in place for packages should not only accommodate change, but should also allow the employer the flexibility to influence package outcomes (e.g. to reduce the ultimate cost by the application of good project management).

Simply having a good provider in place with conditions of contract which enable the management of change is unlikely to be enough to achieve optimum

---

[10] Bernice L. Roque, B. L. (n.d.) *PMP, Enabling Effective Project Sponsorship: A Coaching Framework for Starting Projects Well*.

APM Guide to Contracts and Procurement

success. It also takes competent people, supported by good operational systems and a supportive organisational environment to optimally manage a contracted-out package. In addition to having generic project management competencies, the effective project manager managing outsourced packages needs to:

- Have background knowledge of the applicable contract law.
- Have specific knowledge of the applicable conditions of contract.
- Have an understanding of the range of potential consequences of their decisions and actions more so than for a non-contractual environment.
- Be able to communicate with precision in order to give the provider clear direction and to avoid some common pitfalls that can lead to delays, additional costs and poor quality of the final deliverables.

This guide has been developed based on the real-world experience of the members of the APM's Contracts and Procurement SIG and is intended to provide an easy to use reference source for project managers who are involved in more complex projects that have a significant outsourced content.

1.1.4 The 'agile' perspective

A relatively recent development is the advent of 'agile' project delivery methods.

The *Agile Manifesto* was written in February 2001 at Utah at a summit of practitioners of software methodologies. The manifesto promotes a number of key values (see Figure 1.5).

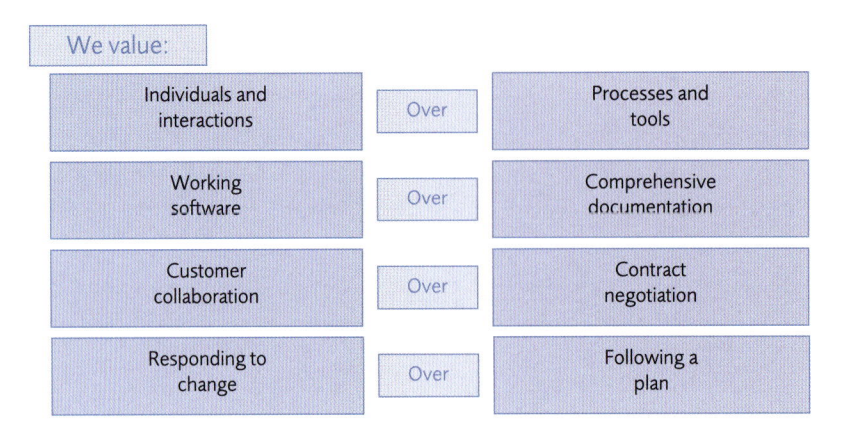

We value:		
Individuals and interactions	Over	Processes and tools
Working software	Over	Comprehensive documentation
Customer collaboration	Over	Contract negotiation
Responding to change	Over	Following a plan

Figure 1.5 The 'agile' values

Introduction

Much has been written already about the agile approach, which is a method mainly used for software development in the IT sector. It is also being migrated to be used in other sectors (e.g. electronic product development). The main reason for the emergence of agile is the fast pace of innovation and development in the related industries, where technology does not remain static for more than a few months.

Research has been conducted[11] into the contracting of work that utilises agile methodologies and this area is still in development.

From a procurement perspective, a capped or rolling input-based contracting basis under a framework or main body contract (see Chapter 4 for further description) is commonly used to account for a defined number of agile 'iterations' planned. The contract main body may define the background terms such as; parties to the contract, IP ownership, security, jurisdiction, materials mark-up and labour rates; an annexed statement of work (SoW) may thoroughly detail the ways of working for the form of agile methodology selected.

'Agile contracting' being an area subject to further development, is not covered in depth in this guide. The APM Contracts and Procurement SIG is planning to provide a specific publication to cover this aspect in the future.

1.2 How to use this guide

The reader may be at the beginning of the procurement life cycle; in which case, we recommend that he/she should read through the full guide. We strongly recommend that the early stages of the life cycle (e.g. concept and feasibility stage and project procurement strategy stage) are extremely valuable; as decisions made during these early stages have a large impact on the follow-on stages. Too often, a lack of thought here effectively sinks a project.

Alternatively, the reader may be taking over a contract at an intermediate stage in which case he/she may jump to the specific stages necessary to quickly understand the key points for urgent consideration. The stage overviews are provided at the beginning of each of Chapters 2–8 to enable the reader to quickly decide which stage in the cycle he/she is at and which chapters should be the priority.

The depth of the process required will vary significantly depending on the size and complexity of the overall project and the potential impact of what is being procured on the success of the project or programme.

---

[11] Ganes and Naevdal (2008) NTNU Thesis.

APM Guide to Contracts and Procurement

1.3 Key term definitions used in this guide

The key terms that are used throughout this guide are defined below.

Procurement: Procurement is the process by which the benefits, enhanced capability, functions/performance or resources (goods and services) required from or by a project or programme are acquired.[12]

It includes deciding the package breakdown structure (PaBS)[13] and, for each package, the development and implementation of:

- a contracting strategy;
- contract documents, including the specific scope/requirement; and
- process and evaluation criteria for selection and award.

These lead to the effective management and administration of the contracts once entered into.

Employer: The party that instigates the contract and that will pay the consideration, usually monetary, to the provider on delivery of the requirement which meets the defined acceptance criteria.

Provider: Any of:

- A manufacturer supplying standard goods.
- A manufacturer designing and/or manufacturing goods to an employer's unique requirement, whether it is a one-off deliverable or thousands of units.
- A consultancy organisation providing professional services, whether these are 'business-as-usual' services (e.g. accountancy), or project specific services.

---

[12] Of course, the benefits and enhanced capabilities accruing from the completed project cannot be acquired directly from the providers but it is such benefits and capabilities that are the essence of why the project is being undertaken. Hence, we emphasise the benefits and capabilities here and elsewhere in this guide.

[13] We define below the PaBS and why it is defined as different from the WBS. Note that we are not wishing to invent a new acronym for the sake of it. There is a distinct difference in the context of project procurement.

- An outsourcing organisation providing ongoing services tailored to the employer's specific needs.
- A party delivering a works contract, whether the requirement is expressed contractually as a fully specified design, performance or functional specification, a new or enhanced capability or a business benefit.

Contract: A legally enforceable agreement between two or more parties defining the obligations of each party. It specifies:

- The deliverables (which may be in the form of levels of performance), called the requirement in this guide, that it is necessary for the provider to deliver to meet its obligations.
- The corresponding consideration, normally monetary, that the employer will pay to the provider in return for the requirements once delivered.

In a project environment, in which there is a defined life cycle, as opposed to a simple transactional contract for pre-manufactured goods, the procurement process should yield, as a minimum, for inclusion in this contract:

- The constraints under which the requirement is to be delivered.
- How the contract is to be administered (e.g. project management requirements, points of contact, payment terms, change control, etc.).
- The consideration to be paid to the provider against the deliverables.
- The acceptance criteria for the deliverables.
- Remedies for non-performance.

Requirement: The technical definition of the level of performance to be achieved by the delivered solution and the constraints under which it is to be delivered and must operate.

Package: Part of a project that can be packaged as a single component part of the overall project and may be outsourced.

Goods: The standard manufactured items, which have little or no uniqueness about them. They can be bought 'off the shelf'.

Services: The standard services which are incidental to the delivery of a project. They can be for year on year services like accounting, legal services etc.

APM Guide to Contracts and Procurement

Works: The combination of goods and services within a project or part of a project. This can be both for services to deliver a unique output e.g. a building design; a tailored ongoing service e.g. an outsourcing arrangement; or a physical output (goods) e.g. a building.

Package breakdown structure (PaBS): The PaBS is a structure formed to break down the overall project into elements that can be considered as deliverables (the structure being analogous to a work breakdown structure (WBS) – see definition below). The PaBS divides the works, to whatever level defined, into packages which can be individually sourced, being either allocated to internal parts of the employer organisation or let under contract to external providers. The elements of the PaBS may contain some of those of a WBS; grouped together where they can be provided by a single provider, forming a 'package' to be contracted to provide the associated benefits. Note that, while the whole project is not being contracted out, the overall outcomes and benefits may be pivotal on some contracted packages being (1) correctly/completely specified and (2) successfully delivered.

> **Work breakdown structure (WBS):** A way in which a project may be divided by level into discrete groups for programming, cost planning and control purposes. The WBS is a tool for defining the hierarchical breakdown of work required to deliver the products of a project. Major categories are broken down into smaller components. These are sub-divided until the lowest level of detail is established. The WBS defines the total work to be undertaken on the project and provides a structure for all project control systems.

The PaBS, therefore, goes beyond a WBS in defining the reasons for the existence of the deliverables including, for each element identified:

1: The higher-level elements of outcomes and benefits;[14]
2: The success criteria, which may define the project's outputs;
3: The new or enhanced capabilities, which in engineering terms may be expressed as a requirement specification; and
4: The goods and services needed.

[14] We emphasise that when contracting significant parts of a project to providers the overall outcomes and benefits of the endeavour need to be considered. Ask the question: 'Does this contract support the overall outcomes and benefits of the project or programme and is there anything to add to maintain/support them?'

2
Concept and feasibility

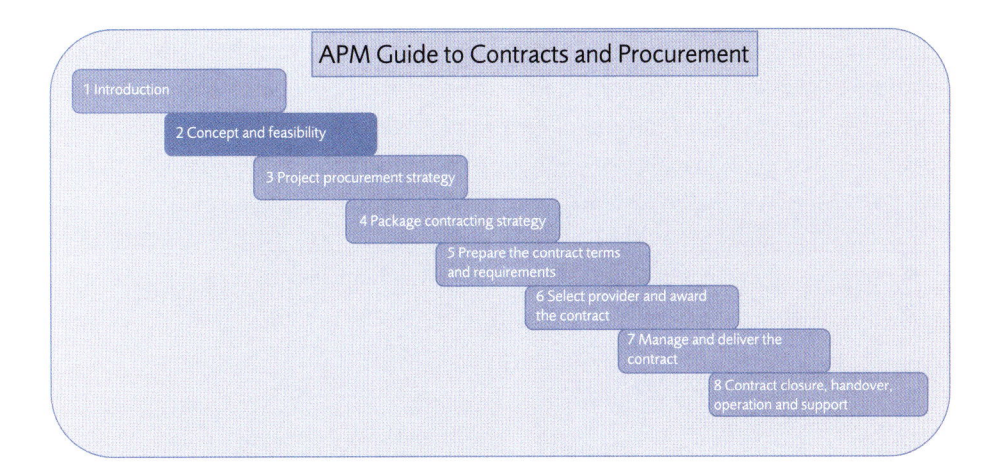

APM Guide to Contracts and Procurement
- 1 Introduction
- 2 Concept and feasibility
- 3 Project procurement strategy
- 4 Package contracting strategy
- 5 Prepare the contract terms and requirements
- 6 Select provider and award the contract
- 7 Manage and deliver the contract
- 8 Contract closure, handover, operation and support

2.0 Overview

This chapter describes the concept and feasibility stage, being a precursor to all the follow-on stages of the procurement life cycle. It determines whether the proposed project is viable and in what form. Rushing into the procurement process (e.g. due to imposed time-pressures) and then finding that contracts need to be significantly modified or even aborted can have major cost, time and quality impacts. The concept and feasibility stage asks the question:

'Do I fully understand why this project needs to go ahead and what the expected benefits will be?'

It therefore goes beyond the scope of procurement and examines:

- **Is it a worthwhile undertaking?** Will it contribute benefits in line with the sponsoring organisation's mission and strategy for an adequate period of time to make it worthwhile? The benefits and the applicable success criteria must be defined in order to assess this.
- **Is it feasible and practicable?** Is it feasible to undertake and deliver within the assigned budget, timescale and other constraints identified? Can a supply chain deliver what is required (is the required capability available)? It must be

feasible and practicable for the defined benefits to be delivered within the budget, time and quality constraints applied. As part of this assessment, a number of different delivery options may be identified, explored and, in many cases, discarded. The option(s) found to be sufficiently feasible and practicable will be put forward as the optimum way(s) of satisfying the identified need.

Activities during the concept and feasibility stage are towards developing a 'full' business case as a key output along with the decision to proceed with the project or not. Business case development commences with the generation of an outline version, which we term the 'strategic' business case (SBC), which is developed to become the 'full' business case (FBC) at the end of the stage.[15]

Beyond the decision to proceed with the project or not, the primary output of the concept and feasibility stage will be the 'full' business case (FBC) document.

2.1 Background

The concept and feasibility stage examines the whole reasoning for going ahead with a particular project and includes considering whether contracting with external providers is part of the delivery strategy. The key outputs from the stage are therefore answers to:

1. Should we proceed with the project at all?
2. Should we consider using contracted providers?
3. Can a supply chain deliver?

Proceeding with the next stage of a procurement life cycle is dependent on the answers being 'yes' to questions 1 and 2. When the answers are 'yes', the findings of this stage will be captured in the FBC as a key output.

The work undertaken during this stage is subject to development and refinement in the follow-on stages. Where large elements of a project are to be contracted-out, the generation of options and the assessment of each option's feasibility is best assessed with involvement of the project delivery resources, including project management, procurement, technical subject matter experts

---

[15] In this chapter, we have used the terms SBC and FBC to differentiate the content at the start and the end of the business case development process. The FBC is generally termed simply as the 'business case' for the purposes of the ongoing project.

Concept and feasibility

and even potential providers (if it does not undermine future competition). Indeed, 'early contractor involvement' (ECI) clauses have been added to the industry-standard NEC3 standard form of contract[16] due to the perceived benefits this provides to contract delivery. The desirability of having these people involved is partly why we have included 'concept and feasibility' phase in this guide. The two other main reasons are:

- A trend towards contracts where the provider is paid against improved performance at business level i.e. for benefits/outcomes which are defined in the outputs from this stage; and
- Starting with a poor business case will cause change later which will be especially expensive once in contract. A changing or knowingly ill-defined business case needs to be reflected in the project procurement strategy to avoid unnecessary expense and delay.

2.2 Inputs

The primary inputs at this stage are:

- An identified need or opportunity.
- A defined corporate strategy or plan.

Projects are undertaken to fulfil a business need or opportunity which will ultimately provide benefit to an organisation. The role of project management is to undertake projects that deliver agreed benefits to an organisation. Hence, in defining the business need or opportunity, a link with the defined corporate strategy is imperative. It would be wasteful to instigate a project that is irrelevant or which does not contribute to corporate strategy and clearly it would be counter-productive to instigate one that is at odds with it.

2.3 Activities

The activities undertaken during the concept and feasibility stage, as illustrated in Figure 2.1, are as follows:

[16] NEC (2015) *Early Contractor Involvement* (ECI).

APM Guide to Contracts and Procurement

1. Develop the 'strategic' business case (SBC).
2. Gain support of a business case sponsor.
3. Identify and analyse stakeholders.
4. Decide which stakeholders to engage with and when.
5. Assess stakeholder views in order to:
   a. Develop the project brief.
   b. Identify and develop the high-level options and produce the options paper.
   c. Estimate the overall project cost in the context of the overall endeavour.
6. Assess and Select the best option(s), involving key stakeholders in the process.
7. Develop a project scope statement for the preferred option(s) including an initial budget and an overall programme plan with contingencies.
8. Refine/update the SBC, including budget, programme plan and contingencies.
9. Conduct a gateway review in order to obtain a decision on whether to proceed with the project or not, and if it is a medium or major project for organisation; (9a) involve the future project board/steering group.

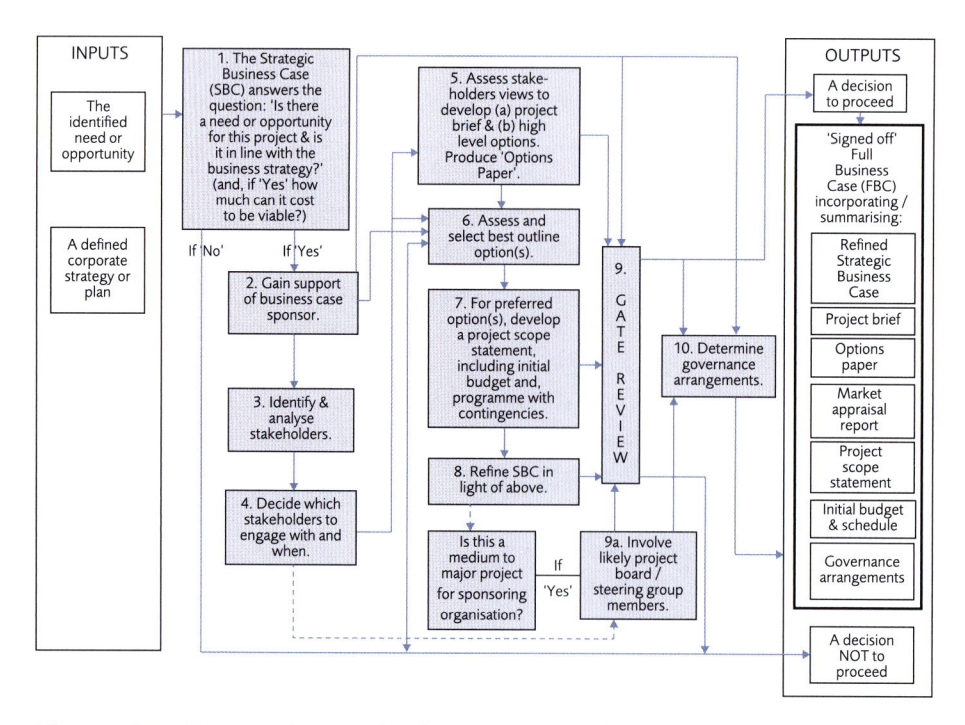

Figure 2.1 Process diagram for the concept and feasibility stage

Concept and feasibility

10. Determine the governance arrangements: If the size of the project warrants it then appoint a project sponsor and project board/steering group (if not already in place) and re-visit activity 9.

To do this, resources are needed to undertake the stage, including ensuring early involvement of the expected delivery team (e.g. project manager and procurement resources).

2.3.1 Activity 1: Develop the 'strategic' business case (SBC)

Once a need or opportunity is identified, an SBC should be developed, the purpose of which is to demonstrate that the opportunity is both viable and in line with the corporate business strategy. By viable, we mean that once the project is delivered, it will continue to deliver benefit to the sponsoring organisation and other stakeholders for a period of time that makes it a worthwhile undertaking.

> **Business case:** The business case provides justification for undertaking a project or programme. It evaluates the benefit, cost and risk of alternative options and the rationale for the preferred solution. *APM Body of Knowledge 6th edition*

The *APM Body of Knowledge* (6th edition) provides an overview of what is generally contained in a business case.[17] At a high level, this SBC needs to show:

- What the need or opportunity is.
- The strategic fit – how it fits within the corporate business strategy and/or within a programme or portfolio of projects.
- The main business benefits to be achieved.
- The sensitivities of any forecasts or estimates, e.g. will the business case figures stand up in 12/24 months' time? Are they based on certain assumptions? What intelligence can procurement/specialists provide around things like material indices, exchange rates, oil prices, etc., which may affect the future viability of the business case?

---

[17] APM (n.d.) *APM Body of Knowledge* 6th edition, section 3.1.1.

APM Guide to Contracts and Procurement

> **Benefit:** The quantifiable and measurable improvement resulting from completion of deliverables that is perceived as positive by a stakeholder. It will normally have a tangible value, expressed in monetary terms that will justify the investment. *APM Body of Knowledge 6th edition*

It is desirable for the business benefits to be quantified, although in some cases it may not be possible to quantify these fully at this early stage. It is, however, essential to identify the following in the SBC:

- The affordability criteria: usually determined by a cost/benefit analysis. This needs to take a 'whole-life' view of the expenditure and the benefits over the life of the facility/service including its disposal and through-life upgrades as appropriate.
- The principal stakeholders: those who will benefit from the project and those who may be against it.
- The degree of uncertainty associated with the project, particularly in relation to the employer organisation's appetite for risk, experience, ability, knowledge of projects and its current portfolio of projects; the external environment and the delivery of the identified benefits once the project has been delivered. This implies both:
  - an application of risk management methods; and
  - a statement of the assumptions being made, which are in themselves a source of risk.

The required benefits should be documented as part of the required outputs from this stage. This will form an important baseline for the performance of the provider and the ongoing support and operations team to evaluate whether the packages or follow-on operations should be terminated (see section 8.7).

A specific benefits realisation plan[18] document may be necessary for larger or more complex projects or programmes.

2.3.2 Activity 2: Gain support of a business case sponsor

If the SBC has merit, then it should gain the support of an authoritative sponsor for its further development. The sponsor must be someone who can make the decision, or significantly influence the decision, over whether the project will

---

[18] A benefits realisation plan describes the process to be undertaken following completion to evaluate whether the requisite benefits have been achieved.

ultimately go ahead. The sponsor must also have the authority to allocate resources to the further development of the SBC. We use the term 'business case sponsor' as at this stage, the role of project sponsor will not be allocated as no project yet exists; however, when and if the project is sanctioned, it is likely that, in Activity 10, the identified business case sponsor would become the project sponsor.

2.3.3 Activity 3: Identify all stakeholders and analyse

> **Stakeholder:** The organisations or people who have an interest or role in the project, programme or portfolio or are impacted by it. *APM Body of Knowledge 6th edition*

Once the SBC is approved, the wider group of stakeholders should be identified beyond those detailed in the SBC.

> **Stakeholder management:** The systematic identification, analysis, planning and implementation of actions to engage with stakeholders. *APM Body of Knowledge 6th edition*

The analysis should include the likely attitude of stakeholders towards the project, i.e. are they likely to be positive, neutral or negative to it?

Also consider their actual level of influence? Who leads the others' opinions on matters, and who just follows everyone else?

Consider the knowledge and relevant experience within the employer at this stage, because this will determine a number of the following stages and decisions.

2.3.4 Activity 4: Decide which stakeholders to engage with and when

At the concept and feasibility stage, it may simply be impossible to engage with all stakeholders to obtain detailed feedback. Where it is identified that a significant proportion of the work is to be outsourced, potential providers need to be included in the research (see section 2.1 – ECI). It needs to be understood that engaging with external stakeholders may give away some competitive advantage or attract unwarranted attention and publicity (consider using non-disclosure agreements). The stakeholder group may therefore include:

- the ultimate owner of the project deliverables;
- finance, tax, capital allowances experts;
- potential providers where known (ECI);
- end users, including marketing, operations human resources (HR), etc.;
- maintainers; (hard and soft facilities, i.e. soft costs are often far higher than hard costs in the long term, so consider the impact of the project on these as well);
- other personnel with relevant experience; and
- outsourcing for advice if not available within the organisation.

The objectives for the further stakeholder engagement are:

- to develop the project brief; and
- to develop the range of delivery options for the project, which are encapsulated in the options paper.

> **Project brief (brief):** The output of the concept phase of a project or programme. *APM Body of Knowledge 6th edition*

If the appropriate experienced stakeholders are not available within the organisation then external input will be required, for example, subject matter experts on certain trades, designers or cost consultants. As noted above, this external engagement may need to be carefully managed to avoid giving away competitive advantage.

2.3.5 Activity 5: Assess stakeholder views

Activity 5 'Assess stakeholder views' is discussed in two sections to cover the development of the project brief and an options paper, if required.

2.3.5.1 Activity 5a: Assess stakeholder views to develop the project brief

This will include the possible benefits flowing from the completed project being developed to give clear, concise and precise objectives for a completed project, which in turn can be expressed as measurable success criteria.

Concept and feasibility

> **Success criteria:** The qualitative or quantitative measures by which the success of P3 management is judged. *APM Body of Knowledge 6th edition*

Success criteria that are expressed qualitatively can often be arranged on a scale or ladder to judge relative success. In some cases, the employer may be able to contract with a provider who is wholly or partly rewarded on the achievement of these success criteria.

The necessary stakeholder consultation needed to develop the project brief can be as follows:

- Internal stakeholders can be consulted directly.
- External stakeholders may be consulted in a number of ways, which could include:
  - face-to-face conversations;
  - questionnaires;
  - RFIs (requests for information) to potential providers; and
  - discussion groups.

In addition, at this stage, the most likely views of the more influential external stakeholders should be taken into account, even if they are not consulted, as they could significantly affect the project in a detrimental way. For instance, on a new-build road project, environmentalists may raise significant objections to the proposed project, which may, if not overcome, add significant cost and cause time delay to the project.

Some other factors to consider include 'buildability' and resource availability.

2.3.5.2 Activity 5b: Assess stakeholder views to develop the options paper

Much of what could be said here would repeat what is said for Activity 5a. The key difference is that having now established a high level specification of the end customers' needs and wants, the focus switches to identifying and evaluating, at a high level, the different options to deliver these objectives, which may require early provider involvement. For instance, if, for a manufacturing company with constrained capacity, the objective is 'to sell new product X at a profit before the competition launches a similar product', then the options could be:

APM Guide to Contracts and Procurement

- build a new factory unit either adding to existing premises or at another location;
- stop manufacturing an older product and use the capacity to build new product X; or
- subcontract the manufacture of product X to an external organisation, either wholly or partly and if partly, taking account of how it is to be integrated or assembled, etc.

All of these approaches will have strengths and weaknesses as well as opportunities and threats, which need to be identified and evaluated. A SWOT matrix[19] can be a useful tool to assess these factors (see the example of Figure 2.2).

Some of these options will naturally drop away as not feasible, unrealistic, too risky or unaffordable; leaving those that are the most suitable for consideration.

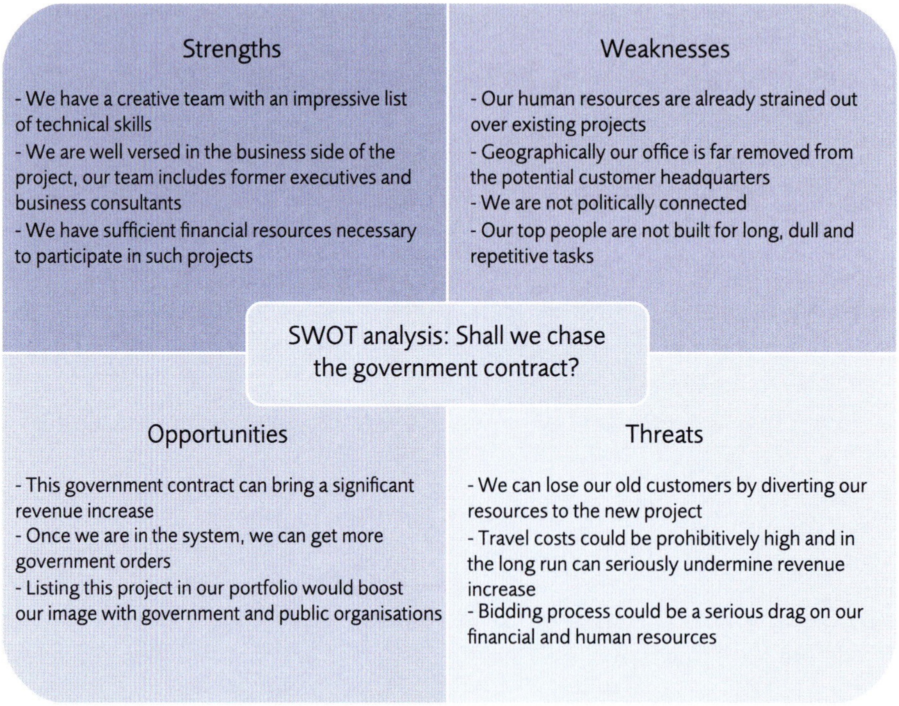

Strengths	Weaknesses
- We have a creative team with an impressive list of technical skills - We are well versed in the business side of the project, our team includes former executives and business consultants - We have sufficient financial resources necessary to participate in such projects	- Our human resources are already strained out over existing projects - Geographically our office is far removed from the potential customer headquarters - We are not politically connected - Our top people are not built for long, dull and repetitive tasks

SWOT analysis: Shall we chase the government contract?

Opportunities	Threats
- This government contract can bring a significant revenue increase - Once we are in the system, we can get more government orders - Listing this project in our portfolio would boost our image with government and public organisations	- We can lose our old customers by diverting our resources to the new project - Travel costs could be prohibitively high and in the long run can seriously undermine revenue increase - Bidding process could be a serious drag on our financial and human resources

Figure 2.2 SWOT matrix

[19] SWOT: strengths, weaknesses, opportunities and threats analysis: Origin obscure.

Tools such as internal rate of return (IRR)[20] can assist this judgement by providing quantified return on investment (ROI).[21]

To assess the remaining options objectively, it is often useful to consult people who have some experience of delivering similar options and, in some cases, it may be worthwhile to commission these personnel to do specialist assessments. For example, to use a cost consultant to develop approximate costs for each option in the form of a market appraisal report, showing expected supply and demand characteristics for the planned project and any impact this may have.

One of the options that should always be considered is the 'do nothing' or 'not proceed with this project' option. This may be because the costs or timescales for the identified delivery options may not make it worthwhile for it to proceed. Alternatively, it may not be chosen to proceed because, whilst shown to be worthwhile, there may be other more beneficial projects in which the organisation can invest. In short, if you are to kill a project, kill it early to avoid unnecessary costs being spent on it.

For each of the feasible outline options, their high level advantages and disadvantages, including any threats or opportunities leading to additional benefits and the likely whole life costs, should be identified and assessed.

At this stage when considering using provider(s) we recommend reviewing of the kind of employer–provider power balance relationship that could result and understanding the pitfalls (see section 3.3.6).

Industry-specific process guidance on how to evaluate and determine the potential options may be available. Some examples for various industry sectors are:

- In the construction industry RICS has produced the *New Rules of Measurement* (NRM) series,[22] the Royal Institute of British Architects (RIBA) has produced the *Plan of Work 2013*[23] and Office of Government Commerce

---

[20] IRR source: Internal Rate of Return: The rate of return that makes the net present value of all cash flows (positive and negative) from a particular investment equal zero.

[21] ROI: Return on Investment: The benefit to an investor resulting from an investment of resources. It has been argued that this should be used as the benchmark against which all projects should be ultimately evaluated – see: http://www.jonbroome.com/blog/february-2016/roce-what's-that-got-to-do-with-project,-programme.

[22] RICS (2013) *New Rules of Measurement*.

[23] RIBA (2013) *Plan of Work 2013*.

(OGC) has produced *Gateway Process* publications[24] as industry-recognised frameworks.
- In the IT industry the British Computer Society (BCS) has produced *A Practitioner's Guide to Selection and Procurement*.[25]
- In the defence industry the UK Ministry of Defence (MOD) has produced *Better Defence Acquisition*.[26]

The findings are incorporated into the options paper including those options that have been considered and discarded and the reasons why. Being able to share this information with providers later can come in useful in improving how we procure and support defence equipment.

2.3.6 Activity 6: Assess and select the best outline option(s)

The delivery options identified in the options paper should be assessed against the benefits, objectives and success criteria defined in the project brief. This assessment can be effected as part of a down-selection meeting, which brings together the key stakeholders to debate the merits of the tabled options. Note that there should be no surprises at this meeting due to the involved stakeholders being consulted during the development of the project brief and the options paper. There may be a clear 'winning' option, or it may be difficult to choose from several, in which case the procurement resource should be further engaged to do further research, which needs to be resourced accordingly.

The output from the down-selection meeting and the preceding activities are summarised in the down-selection meeting minutes, confirming the decision to proceed. Formal sign-off should be by the 'acting' business case sponsor (whether formally appointed or not).

For a medium to major project within an organisation, it is likely that some of the key stakeholders will go on to form the project board or steering group; assuming the project is fully sanctioned to go ahead.

---

[24] OGC (n.d.) *Gateway Process* publications.
[25] Tate, M. (2015) BCS *A Practitioner's Guide to Selection and Procurement*.
[26] UK Ministry of Defence (2013) *Better Defence Acquisitions*.

Concept and feasibility

2.3.7 Activity 7: Develop project scope statement for the preferred option(s)

The project scope statement(s) are developed based on the preferred delivery option(s) identified.

> **Scope:** The totality of the outputs, outcomes and benefits and the work required to produce them. *APM Body of Knowledge 6th edition*

A scope statement document would typically include:

- What is within the scope of the project, what is outside of the scope and what has yet to be decided as either inside or outside of scope; and who wants or needs to have control over the design/specification? NB: These factors will affect the choice of contract and the choice of procurement route in subsequent stages.
- Other high level boundaries or constraints acting on the project: practically all projects have a time deadline; however there may be additional constraints. For example, for a road upgrade project, there may be environmental constraints particular to that project and the requirement to keep traffic flowing on an existing road during construction. For an IT project, it could be the need for compatibility with other systems.
- A high-level work breakdown structure sufficient to provide an initial estimate of costs. At this stage, approximate estimates may be used but should also specify the estimation accuracy. In the construction industry, this is now generally referred to as an 'order of cost estimate' by RICS; since the 2014 New Rules of Measurement were introduced.
- A suitably detailed risk assessment, identifying risks and opportunities and listing outline containment actions for risks and the enabling activities for opportunities.

Based on all of the above, an initial budget and schedule with contingencies should be developed for incorporation into the FBC.

2.3.8 Activity 8: Refine the strategic business case

In the light of all the above activities, the case for – or against – the project should have become clearer as more stakeholders are consulted and the project's definition has evolved. In particular, the benefits will have been refined and confirmed; initial assumptions clarified and confirmed; risks and opportunities quantified. In addition, some time will have passed, which may have caused changes in the needs or opportunities that the project addresses. As a result, it makes sense to refine and update the initial SBC prior to the project's first formal gate review.

2.3.9 Activity 9: Gate review

> **Gate review (gate):** The point between phases, gates and/or tranches where a go/no go decision can be made about the remainder of the work.
> *APM Body of Knowledge 6th edition*

Within project execution, periodic gate reviews provide a health check on the project. A gate review will have defined pass and fail criteria, which will be dependent upon the project stage in which the gate review occurs. Usually each gate review will determine whether approval to proceed is given and the necessary release of funding and other resources to proceed to the next stage.

The business case owner and project board/steering group, if applicable, should have been briefed and provided feedback in the main activities leading up to the gate review, including having taken part in Activity 6 (section 2.3.6), where the best delivery option(s) were chosen. Indeed, if two or more competing options were taken forward from Activity 6, this may be where – after further refinement and development – the single best one is formally selected.

Gate reviews are formal points in a project where its overall expected worth, the progress made, cost incurred, and the forward execution plan are reviewed and a decision made whether to continue with the next phase or stage of the project. Consequently, at the conclusion of each gate review the project sponsor should sign-off whether the project is to continue in its current form, be modified or culled. Mature project-based organisation will have defined what these are for all projects, although the number and rigour of each review may vary depending on the value, risk etc. of the project.

Concept and feasibility

2.3.10 Activity 10: Determine governance arrangements

> **Governance:** The set of policies, regulations, functions, processes, procedures and responsibilities that define the establishment, management and control of projects, programmes or portfolios. *APM Body of Knowledge 6th edition*

Governance of project management is about the high-level monitoring of the progress of a project or programme towards the delivery of its defined benefits. Note that benefits are considered, as part of the governance role, to ensure that any changes to the operational environment are considered. This potentially means adjusting the project objectives to fit the external world – a change which should not be taken lightly at the whim of the project manager or the project sponsor. Any such change should be subject to the change control process and due governance.

Whatever the project's objectives are, the progress towards them made by the project team needs to be monitored. There are three primary tiers of governance.

The first tier of governance is that provided by the project sponsor.

> **Project sponsor (sponsorship):** An important senior management role. The sponsor is accountable for ensuring that the work is governed effectively and delivers the objectives that meet identified needs. *APM Body of Knowledge 6th edition*

The project sponsor must be someone with the appropriate authority to make things happen and with a personal commitment to the project's success, being a conduit between the project team and the wider organisation. The project sponsor steers the project team based on feedback from the wider organisation and acts as champion for the project. In later stages, this could include 'defending' it against unnecessary change from stakeholders. The project sponsor will also periodically monitor performance of the project; sanctioning, if appropriate, significant corrective actions.

As such, the project sponsor should have regular periodic contact with the project team (for example, on a monthly basis), but does not – and should not – need to be involved in its day-to-day management, this being the role of the project manager.

The second tier of governance is the project board or steering group.

> **Project board (board):** A body that provides sponsorship to a project, programme or portfolio. The board will represent financial, provider and user interests. *APM Body of Knowledge 6th edition*

The project board will also have the performance of the project reported to them, will sanction any significant decisions, would typically formally meet on a regular basis (e.g. monthly or three-monthly), and would also be party to the gate reviews. The regular meeting schedule should not preclude more frequent informal communications with one or more of the board members as required.

For small projects, relative to the size of the organisation, it may not be worthwhile having a project board in which case the project manager would report directly to the project sponsor.

The last tier of governance operates at corporate level, being primarily concerned with portfolios, major programmes and projects, including those currently under way and those being considered as opportunities. At this level there may be numerous worthwhile projects, some of which cannot be funded, so the governance will largely concern prioritisation.

2.4 Outputs

The outputs from the concept and feasibility stage will consist of:

- A decision to proceed with the project or not.
- A full business case, as defined in section 2.4.1 below.
- The lessons learnt from this stage, particularly including the reasons for rejection of the delivery options considered and rejected.
- Market appraisal report, if created, showing expected supply and demand characteristics for the planned project and any impact this may have.

2.4.1 The 'full' business case

The 'full' business case (FBC) is the documented justification for undertaking the project, in terms of evaluating benefits (translated into objectives and success criteria for the completed project), the costs and risks of alternative options and the rationale for the preferred solution. Its purpose is to obtain management commitment and approval for investment in the project. The FBC will be owned by the project sponsor and will be known simply as the 'business case' when the project starts. Its specific contents will include:

- an archived project brief (Activity 5a);
- a project options paper (if options have been considered, Activity 5b) together with outcome of any down-selection meeting (Activity 6);
- a project scope statement (Activity 7) including an initial budget and initial schedule;
- an archived SBC (Activity 8); expanded as necessary to include the views of the stakeholders in terms of benefits, success criteria, risks, etc.;
- the determined governance arrangements for the project (Activity 10); and
- the market appraisal report, if developed.

Note that the archived documents should be retained as appendices (marked as 'superseded') to enable later review, as may be necessary, to understand how the FBC was developed.

3

Project procurement strategy

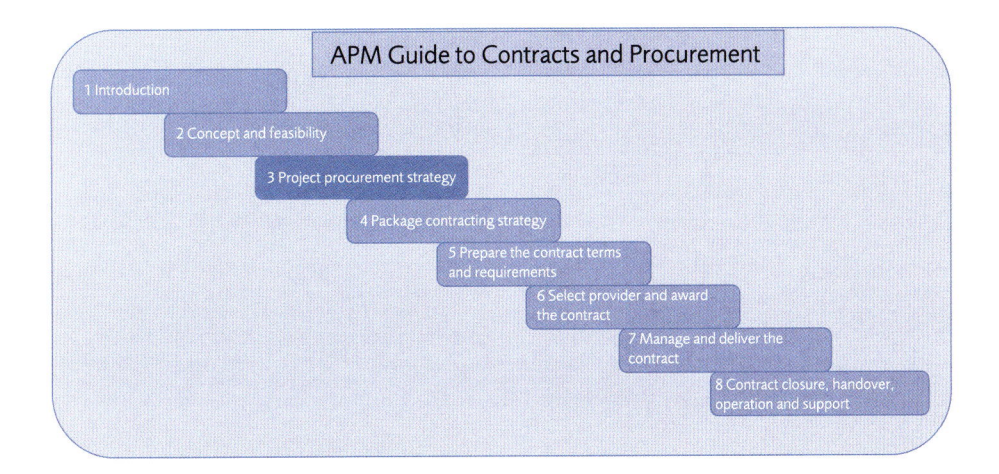

APM Guide to Contracts and Procurement
1 Introduction
2 Concept and feasibility
3 Project procurement strategy
4 Package contracting strategy
5 Prepare the contract terms and requirements
6 Select provider and award the contract
7 Manage and deliver the contract
8 Contract closure, handover, operation and support

3.0 Overview

This chapter describes how to determine the project procurement strategy to be defined in the procurement management plan, which will specify:

- how the overall project is to be broken down into packages;
- which, if any, of these packages may be procured externally; and
- the high-level approach to be taken to procuring each package or category of packages.

To do this, a package breakdown structure (PaBS) is developed to cover the overall project scope, which is then divided into packages that can be considered for procurement.[27] The PaBS is produced via an iterative process that starts with a high-level version which is then refined to produce a final version that is used as

---

[27] See the PaBS definition in section 1.3.

input to the next phase to develop the individual package contracting strategies (Chapter 4) and selection processes (Chapter 6).

During this stage the provider possibilities for the PaBS are considered to determine the scope for outsourcing of the packages, via consultation where necessary, and to understand the 'make or buy' criteria, i.e. whether they are to be sourced internally (via new development or manufacturing) or whether sourced externally.

For each package that will be sourced externally, the stage determines:

- The nature of the relationship to be sought with the potential provider, e.g. where along the collaborative–transactional spectrum each package needs to sit.
- The most appropriate high-level contracting strategy, e.g. cost plus, fixed price, etc.
- The provider selection strategy to be employed, e.g. quality or cost driven.

Once these decisions have been made a detailed procurement schedule, which informs and is informed by the overall project schedule, is developed.

The output of the stage is a procurement management plan document forming a summary of the decisions made and the underlying reasoning to feed into the next phase.

3.1 Background

During the project procurement strategy stage, the project definition is developed to enable decisions to be made regarding what parts of the project (the packages) to develop or make internally and what parts to source externally, i.e. 'make or buy'. This work needs to be driven by the employer's team but outside parties may also be consulted (e.g. prospective providers) or utilised, e.g. consultants. At the end of this stage, the scope of each package should have been largely defined. For the packages that are to be sourced externally, the nature of the relationship must be decided, including who needs to have responsibility and control over the detail of the requirement. An indication needs to be given of the likely contracting strategy, e.g. cost plus or fixed price and the selection process and selection criteria to be adopted made up of cost and qualitative factors. Consider also at this point the drivers for potential providers wanting to deliver a package, i.e. why is it attractive to them to be part of the project? Don't assume every potential provider wants to bid.

Project procurement strategy

Consequently, in this stage for a project of any complexity, there should be input from personnel that:

1. Understand procurement issues, e.g. contracting strategies, and particularly if subject to EU procurement legislation, selection processes. Consider whether your organisation has enough internal knowledge and expertise to progress the procurement. If not, you need to hire external experts to advise and/or external specialists to do the work.
2. Have knowledge of the industry sectors and technologies relevant to the project. This is an opportunity for early provider involvement and requests for information (RFIs).

A factor to consider at this stage is the outline budget for the provider selection process. The criticality of the package may well outweigh its expected cost, therefore the outline budget should reflect the views of the team involved in setting the project procurement strategy. The outline selection budget will form an output from this stage and be further refined in the follow-on package contracting strategy stage (see Chapter 4).

Before we proceed, it is worth revisiting the hierarchy of the requirements that illustrates how the project can be broken down; as illustrated in Figure 3.1 (a repeat of Figure 1.2 in section 1.1.2).

A consideration during this stage is how deeply to specify the PaBS. This is because some latitude needs to be allowed for the detailed requirements to be specified during the later stages as further provider dialogue occurs.

Works, at the lowest level of delivery (a combination of goods and services as defined in section 1.3) are often let under contract as a package to produce something unique. For instance, by combining steel, concrete and labour to a defined plan, a distinct structure in a unique location can be produced, e.g. a bridge. Similarly, by combining software and a help desk service, a 'customer relationship management' function may be created.

However, this does not mean, necessarily, that these items have to be specified to this level in the contract. It is often the case that the supply chain has more specialised knowledge and experience than the employer in providing things of the type required: after all, this is perhaps the biggest reason for outsourcing. It may well be more appropriate to specify at the capability level and allow the provider to break the package down to the goods and services level in order to deliver the specified capabilities. These new or enhanced capabilities may be

APM Guide to Contracts and Procurement

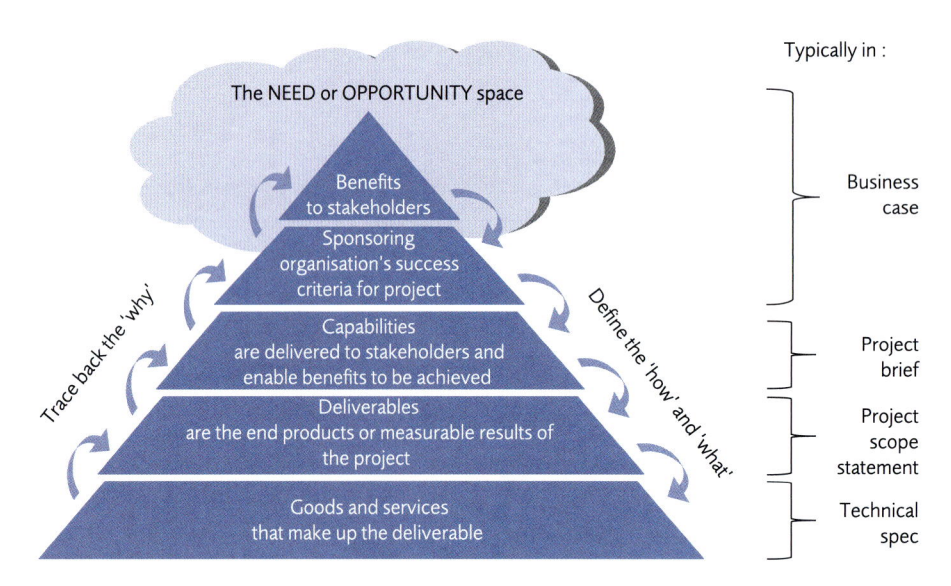

Figure 3.1 The requirements hierarchy expressed in a works contract

defined as performance specifications, if measurable, or alternatively as functional specifications if functional in nature.

Going up a level, the provider may contract on the basis of measures closely related to business outcomes, including the required benefits which are within their control or significant influence, e.g. measurable success criteria. For instance, for a marketing campaign for a product or service the provider may be paid on the basis of increased enquiries to the employer; or for a private finance initiative road project, payment may be linked to the number of journeys along it, average vehicle speed and lane availability. Notice that these are measurable outcomes.

At the project procurement strategy stage, we consider how the project is divided into packages; be they specified in terms of outcomes, satisfied success criteria, new or enhanced capabilities, unique physical works or delivered standard goods and services. The developed procurement strategy will define, for each package: the scope, including how that will be contractually defined, the significant interfaces and interdependencies, and the nature of the relationship being sought. By 'nature of the relationship being sought' we mean direction, at high level, on how the contracted package(s) will be procured in terms of contracting strategy, selection criteria and selection method.

Once defined for all packages or categories of packages, the outputs can be combined or summarised to form a procurement management plan.

Project procurement strategy

3.2 Inputs

In order to decide on the procurement strategy, the outputs from the concept and feasibility stage (see Chapter 2), as included in the FBC, are required.

- The scope statement is critical in order to develop the package breakdown structure (PaBS) to an appropriate level of detail to define individual packages.
- The archived SBC and project brief may also give insight into the sourcing and delivery options considered for the project and the individual work packages within it. It is the starting point for developing criteria by which contracting strategies are developed and providers are selected.

3.3 Activities

The key activities of this phase are illustrated in Figure 3.2 and described in the following sections.

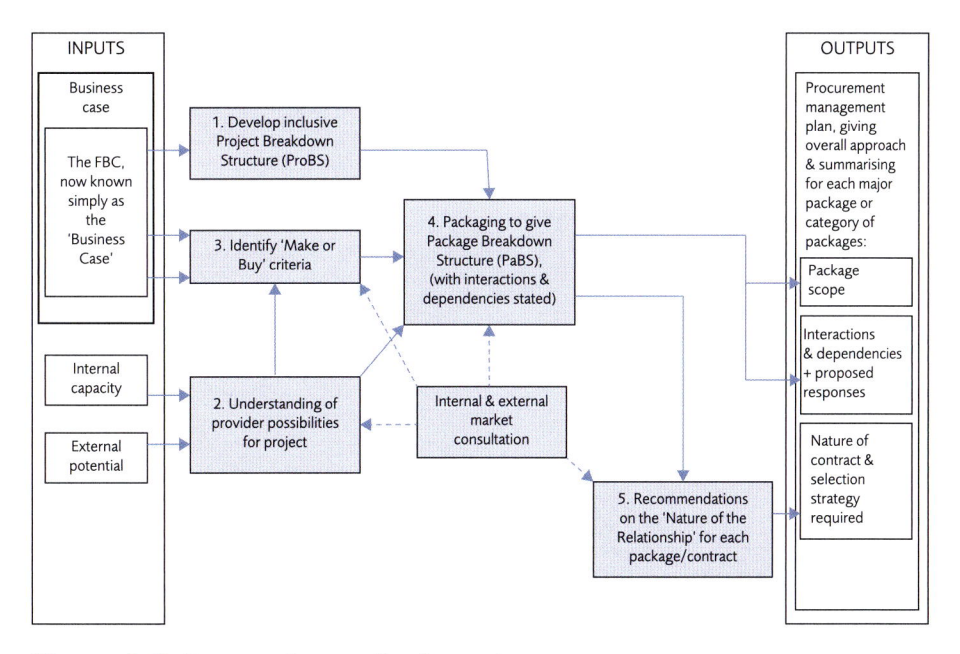

Figure 3.2 Process diagram for the project procurement strategy stage

3.3.1 Internal and external market consultation (ongoing activity)

The extent and formality of consultation with the market will depend on the nature of the project in terms of size, uniqueness, risk, etc. and the existing knowledge of the marketplace within the employer organisation (as well as the constraints under which the employer operates). For instance, if subject to European Union procurement legislation, there is a danger of prejudicing the fair competition requirements if the market is not consulted in an equitable way. Even if EU procurement legislation is not mandated, it is wise to demonstrate fairness in provider selection to avoid reputational damage.

3.3.2 Activity 1: Determine the high-level PaBS

The PaBS is developed via an iterative process, usually starting as relatively high-level and then being refined via consultation. The initial PaBS may be formed by breaking the overall project down into an initial hierarchy by considering the terms as shown in Table 3.1, which uses a solar power station as an example.

Table 3.1 Example high-level package terms for a solar power station

	Example for a solar power station
Business benefits, resulting from the completed project	Quantified increase in revenue and earnings from the completed project. Desired ROCE
Success criteria, by which the project can be judged at the time of its completion	CAPEX (capital expenditure) within budget; completion on or before planned date; initial OPEX (operational expenditure) within budget
Enhanced capabilities that are delivered to the customer organisation(s)	Total power able to be generated, efficiency in terms of converting lumens to power
Deliverables that provide this capability	The design; main construction works including foundations, operator facilities, access roads, solar panels; converters; high-voltage wires connecting to grid, etc.
Work breakdown structure (WBS) of the goods and Services that make up each deliverable.	e.g. For the foundations; holes to be dug, concrete, reinforcing bar, etc.

Project procurement strategy

It may well not be necessary to define the project to the lowest level in the table, but it is necessary to define it to the level at which you will contract for the different packages. And for each level that you go down to, it is critical to identify all the aspects which make up the project, i.e. ensure that the full coverage or breadth of the project is captured. Taking a whole-life view of the project, the requirements for project closure, for support and for ongoing maintenance also need to be included.

> **Summary: Determining the package breakdown structure (PaBS) so far:**
>
> The PaBS, progressively as it is developed, will incorporate:
>
> 1: The higher-level elements of outcomes, specifically considering delivery of the benefits;
> 2: The success criteria, which may define the project's 'hard' objectives;
> 3: The new or enhanced capabilities, which in engineering terms, may be expressed as a performance or functional requirements; and
> 4: The goods and services needed.
>
> It is only when developed to the lowest level of granularity that the hierarchy takes on the form of or indeed becomes like a work breakdown structure (WBS), i.e. where physical or tangible deliverables are defined.

3.3.3 Activity 2: Understanding of provider possibilities for the project

An understanding of the provider possibilities is necessary as it informs the 'make or buy' criteria. It also forms the starting point for intelligent conversations should more detailed market consultation be necessary. This understanding comes from combining knowledge of the internal capacity of the employer organisation with the 'external potential to provide' of the market, as well as its willingness to supply. When making this assessment, it is necessary to understand and take account of any lengthy or critical lead-time requirements which will be inputs to the overall schedule. For example, although a package may be needed at the tail-end of the project, it may have a very long lead-time, and hence might need to be considered early. Alternatively, a long lead item may jeopardise the success of a project (e.g. if the outcome benefits are time-dependent, such as opening a school for the new term or releasing a new piece of IT hardware before Christmas).

The assigned project manager and the assigned procurement professional may already have this knowledge or may need to investigate the internal and external supply base. Whilst this may initially be based on experience and a desktop study, for complex and technologically advanced projects it may be necessary to have wider consultation with the market. A useful exercise here is to issue requests for information (RFIs) or to solicit the expertise of subject matter experts/consultants.

Government procurers need to take care in undertaking market consultation to ensure that it is fair and does not lead to giving any provider(s) a competitive advantage. The whole point of this exercise is to learn from the providers and not to dismiss them at this stage – make sure it is not used to pre-qualify some over others on the basis of limited understanding of what is possible – at this stage it should be all about learning as much as possible. It needs to be driven by an RFI at this stage, not a pre-qualification questionnaire (PQQ; see section 6.4.2).

3.3.4 Activity 3: Identify the 'make or buy' criteria

Analysis of the FBC and the project brief, as well as gaining an understanding of the supply possibilities help identify the criteria by which the 'make or buy'[28] decision can be made. A list of the criteria that might be used is set out in Table 3.2. There may be other criteria dependent on the nature of the project, the industry in which the project is being conducted and the employer organisation's own circumstances.

A key factor in the employer organisation's internal capacity is in terms of skills, functions and capabilities. For instance, if there is an under-utilised internal capability, it may well be in the best interests of the employer organisation to utilise these resources to deliver parts of the project. Those parts that cannot be delivered from within will be sourced from the marketplace requiring the providers that could source them to be assessed. In order to assess what can be delivered externally from providers under contract, the 'external potential to provide' must be explored. It is critical to know what the market is capable of delivering and how external providers could contribute to the project, before the project is divided up into contractual packages (see section 3.3.5), which external providers may be able to supply.

---

[28] An alternative term often used in IT is 'buy or build'.

Table 3.2 Example 'make' or 'buy' criteria

CRITERIA	TEST	EXAMPLE/COMMENT
Criteria 1: Business circumstances		
Financial circumstances	Does buying organisation have to invest in capital to create the product or service?	It may be more cost effective to hire in piece of earth moving equipment rather than buy a new capital item. Note that capital allowances or enhanced capital allowances may be available.
Legislative circumstances	Are there complex standards, practices and procedures that have to be adhered to?	Exacting health and safety procedures may carry risk that cannot be managed.
Criteria 2: Develop and sustain knowledge of the business operation and environment		
Knowledge of the wider organisation	Do we need specialist internal knowledge to be successful?	Understanding the organisation in depth and knowing how it is structured may be a critical factor in providing services.
Culture	Will understanding the culture of the organisation be a critical factor in delivering the products and service?	It may be necessary for the provision of products and services to exhibit particular cultural characteristics e.g. speaking the local language. Are they ready for the change that is coming? Are they used to change?
Criteria 3: Service improvement		
New services	Has our organisation done this before or will we have to invest in building a capability? Do they want to do it?	Projects often involve delivering something new. If the solution is something the organisation has no experience in, then it would be difficult to demonstrate capability, e.g. the use of a new software package or language.
Services difficult to manage or out of control	Are we experts or are others better at delivering what we require?	Requiring an existing capability to deliver service to an exacting service level when there is a track record of not being able to deliver or monitor performance may put a project at risk.
Service level management	Can we deliver to the standards expected?	An internal capability may only be able to deliver 25 widgets a day in one delivery while the project requires 38 delivered just-in-time.

(Continued)

APM Guide to Contracts and Procurement

Table 3.2 *Continued*

CRITERIA	TEST	EXAMPLE/COMMENT
Criteria 4: Effectiveness of delivery		
Availability and effectiveness of internal resources/ capability	Are there internal resources to deliver this effectively?	Internal capacity may not be being utilised yet may have the required track record (reputation for excellence).
Availability and effectiveness of external capacity/ capability	Do others have the capability?	Maybe other suppliers can deliver the service more effectively or are geographically advantaged.
Synergy between product and service	Can a more cost effective solution be delivered if we extend an already existing capability?	It might be possible to bring together two or more services or products into one contract or internal service level agreement thereby creating economies of scale.
Criteria 5: Application of expertise (Note that prior work by Porter – the Five Forces Model[29] explores business strategy against competition and may be helpful in answering the questions below.)		
Strategic value of technical expertise to the organisation	Does the business depend upon a core capability that must be retained or undertaken internally?	If the business undertaking the review provides a unique service or production capability or uses its intellectual property to generate revenue, it is probably better to retain the capability in-house
Technology futures	Is there a technology in the market place that is not available internally?	Maybe an organisation is looking to access new technology or to deploy another's capability to its business advantage where there is no internal expertise.
Criteria 6: Ability to manage risk and contracting		
Contracting risk	Does contracting the package out increase or reduce risk? If the risk is increased, is it justified?	Contacting a work package *always* adds the risks associated with contracting (e.g. provider solvency, legal dispute etc.) but these may be outweighed by the provider's technical experience and competency.
Risk identification	Have the risks associated with the package been identified? Does this need expert input?	When contracting for technical reasons, expert advice may be needed to understand the contracted technical risks.

[29] Porter, M. E. (2008) 'The Five Competitive Forces that Shape Strategy'.

Contractual risk ownership	Has the management ownership of all individual risks been defined? Will organisations that are best placed to manage the risk accept contractual liability for the risk as well i.e. will they be the risk holder?	Once risks are identified the contractual ownership needs to be explicitly defined and acknowledged. This may affect the risk budget allocated (beware of risk double-counting and 'assumed' ownership).

3.3.5 Activity 4: Packaging to give the package breakdown structure (PaBS)[30]

You now divide the PaBS into packages, which can be individually sourced, either internally to parts of the employer organisation or let under contract to external providers.

Having identified what is required, the items need to be packaged into complimentary elements. In doing this, it is possible to identify which packages might be sourced internally, department by department, or externally, e.g. through the new procurement arrangements or using existing framework agreements.

Packaging can be optimised by:

- Bringing similar elements together to gain economies of scale and/or make the package sufficiently attractive to the market. For example, putting supply of all standard electrical components into one package; bringing together all fabrication requirements into one package; or by combining project management and accounting services.
- Combining goods and services into packages, thus giving single point responsibility to a potential provider (or for internal employer organisation's resources if used). The delivery of the packaged goods and services can then be specified as a required performance, functionality or capability.
- Considering and managing the interfaces between packages.

For instance, in construction, the traditional route has been that the functions of design and construction are carried out by separate organisations. This can leave

---

[30] Note: We have not referred to this as the contract breakdown structure as some of the packages may well be procured internally, i.e. there is no contract.

the employer organisation exposed to interfacing problems, e.g. the chosen construction provider may not be able to construct the designed structure. Over the last two decades, there has been a trend for these goods and services to be combined into a single 'design and build' contract package enabling single-point responsibility. For the construction industry, RICS provides a guidance note identifying the different procurement routes that can be followed.[31]

To take the solar power station in Table 3.1 as an example, let us say you have determined from Activity 2 that the solar panel industry, as a sector, is used to performance specifications and has the best organisations to, in competition, determine the number and performance requirements of the solar panels and the supporting electricals, and design and build the concrete bases for the panels to sit on. Consequently, the high-level decision at this stage is that the employer will define, in the contract, the performance/capability requirements and the provider will 'design and build' the rest.

However, from your research, you know that the solar panel sector has no interest or capability in providing, for instance, the access roads on a project of this size and that the small to medium sized construction companies who do this do not normally have design capability. Consequently – although you would not fully define it at this stage – you would have to design the road for them, which is another package. And if you, as an employer, do not have this capability internally, then you will need to develop a contract and selection process for all three packages mentioned: solar panels and ancillaries; road construction and road design. If, on the other hand, you have some design capability for designing roads, then a decision needs to be made against the 'make or buy' criteria.

The concept of packaging is illustrated in Figure 3.3, showing entities that could be sourced separately, but are grouped together into single packages.

An example of a PaBS, being developed based on a project to supply a wind-farm, is illustrated in Figure 3.4.

For more complex projects, which are likely to consist of larger numbers of packages, it is suggested that for each potential package, an initial list should be used to identify for each package:

- what almost certainly will be in it;
- what might be in it; and
- what is not in it.

---

[31] RICS (2014) RICS guidance note, UK Appropriate contract selection 1st edition.

Project procurement strategy

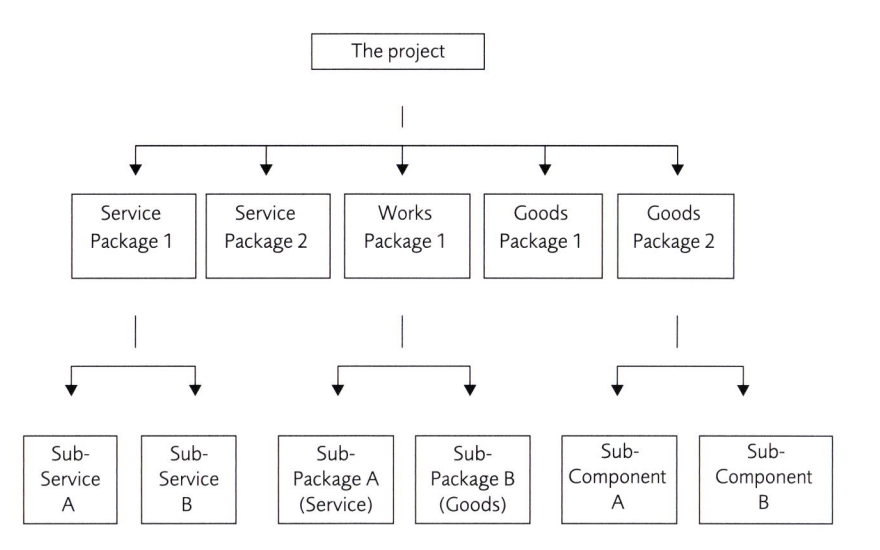

Figure 3.3 Example package breakdown structure (PaBS)

Having gone through a number of iterations with all of the potential packages, the end result should be that every item in the project works hierarchy is in one of the packages, but in one package only, e.g. in terms of goods and services, there is a 'hard' boundary with no duplication or overlap between packages. This should be documented in a scope/responsibility matrix that identifies allocation of ownership for all package components.

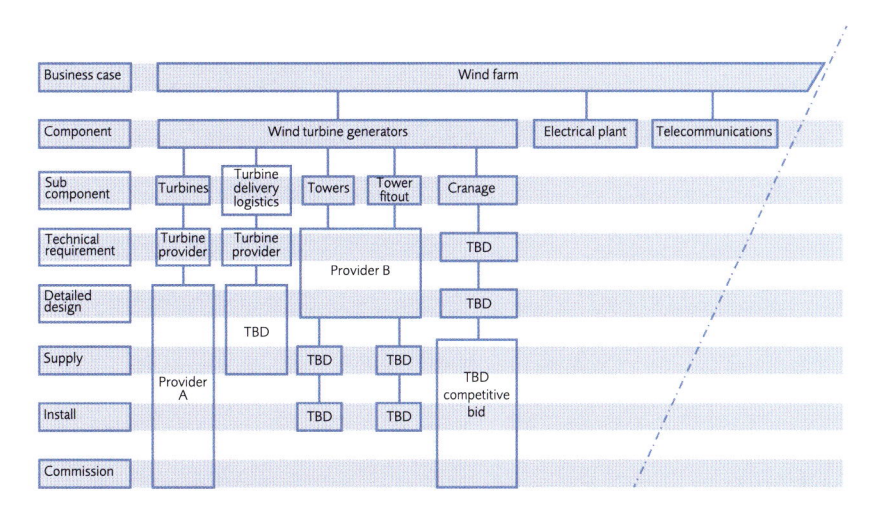

Figure 3.4 PaBS development for a wind-farm project

APM Guide to Contracts and Procurement

Bear in mind that projects are undertaken over a period of time. Consequently, in packaging elements of a project together, the interactions and interdependencies that occur during the implementation phase need to also be considered. As a result, you may decide to package two otherwise separate, but interdependent elements together, so that the chosen provider becomes more motivated to manage the interface successfully. This strategy may reduce the risk of conflict between providers thus reducing the potential for extra management costs for the employer and for the overall project. Taking the 'design and build' example from construction again, another benefit it provides is time-saving; as design and build can more easily overlap if they are in the same package. This is in contrast to the traditional route where design should be finished before the build package is tendered and let.

If it is the employer organisation that will manage these boundaries, then for each package, these interdependencies and interactions must be identified, along with the necessary management steps to ensure smooth delivery. It is worth considering what the provider's tactics may be at these scope boundaries, in order to devise control measures and strategies to prevent such risks occurring. Where less is known, then the provider may charge a premium to manage these risks. Don't think that all risks can be passed to a provider – many are not necessarily better placed to manage the risks than the employer – but you end up paying them for it.

Figure 3.5 illustrates the 'hard' and 'soft' boundaries for goods and services that require definition and management.

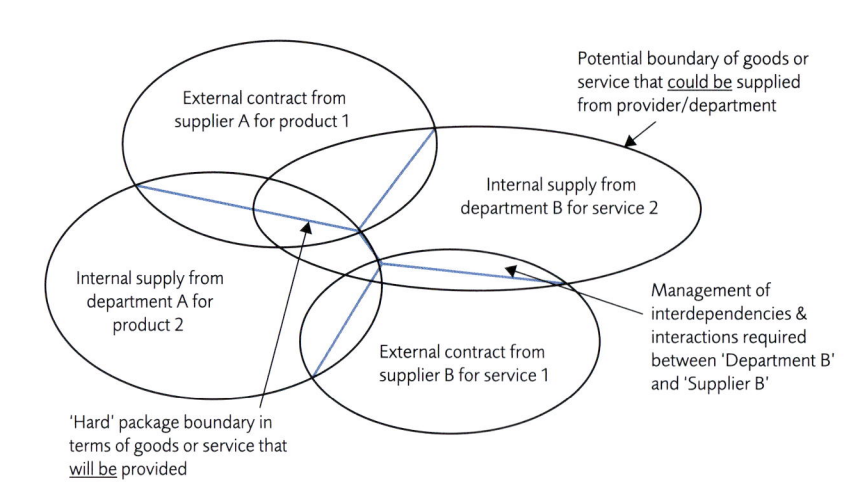

Figure 3.5 The 'hard' and 'soft' boundaries for goods and services

Project procurement strategy

Following putting together an initial PaBS, there may well be a need to consult in greater depth with the market to gain further thoughts on the packaging of the project. It is also possible that the PaBS, as formed, may not be in alignment with what providers may be able and willing to supply. At this stage the project management team may well gain new ideas and perspectives, further understand potential providers' capabilities and have a greater appreciation of the products and services available (i.e. via an RFI). This consultation may result in some activities being revisited and a better or more realistic approach being taken.

3.3.6 Activity 5: Recommendations on the 'nature of relationship' for each contract package

Activity 5 is where the nature of the package is analysed and recommendations made regarding the nature of the employer-supplier relationship. Some factors to be considered are:

1. The type of package with respect to the profit impact and supplier risk. The Kraljic matrix (see Figure 3.6) is a classic procurement model in this respect.

As an example, if the employer is managing the construction of a new building, they might identify that certain components are critical to its operation. For example, for the supply of a lift. As there may not be many lift manufacturers in the world, the employer identifies that in the current market there are long lead-times; with the manufacturers almost being free to name their terms and prices. Consequently, the procurement of the lift is considered a 'strategic' item which needs to be well project managed.

2. The levels of relative investment required by the employer versus the provider which can determine the power balance between them (see Figure 3.7).

Prior study by Bensaou[32] suggests that there is a risk that the provider may have the upper hand once selected based on the relative levels of investment (see inset box below). This factor needs to be understood when deciding on the use of specific providers. Porter, with his 'Five Forces Analysis'[33] considers the factors

---

[32] Bensaou M. (1999) 'Portfolios of Buyer–Supplier Relationships'.
[33] Porter, M. E. (2008) 'The Five Competitive Forces that Shape Strategy'.

Kraljic's Comprehensive Portfolio Approach: Prior study (Kraljic[34]) classifies supplier types into four different categories and identifies the necessary strategies to minimise risk for the buyer. Contracts to deliver something unique will tend to be in the upper half of the diagram, if not the 'strategic' box.

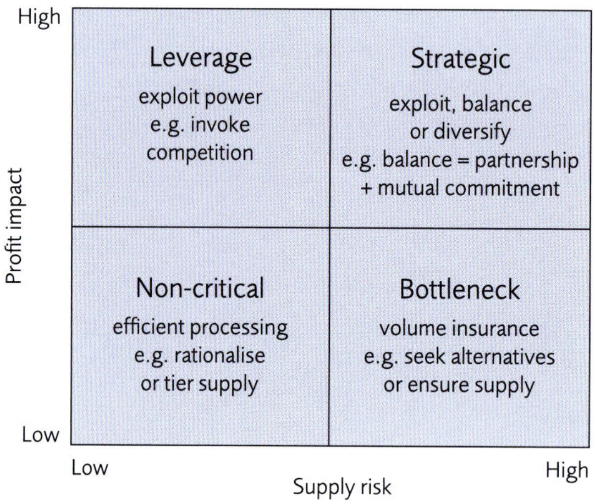

	Low Supply risk	High Supply risk
High Profit impact	**Leverage** exploit power e.g. invoke competition	**Strategic** exploit, balance or diversify e.g. balance = partnership + mutual commitment
Low Profit impact	**Non-critical** efficient processing e.g. rationalise or tier supply	**Bottleneck** volume insurance e.g. seek alternatives or ensure supply

Figure 3.6 Kraljic matrix (Kraljic 1983)

Strategic items (high profit impact, high supply risk): These items deserve the most attention from purchasing managers. Options include developing long-term supply relationships, analysing and managing risks regularly, planning for contingencies, and considering whether to make the item in-house rather than buying it.

Bottleneck items (low profit impact, high supply risk): Useful approaches here include over-ordering when the item is available (lack of reliable availability is one of the most common reasons that supply is unreliable), and looking for ways to control vendors.

Leverage (high profit impact, low supply risk): Purchasing approaches to consider here include using your full purchasing power, substituting products or suppliers, and placing high-volume orders.

Non-critical (low profit impact, low supply risk): Purchasing approaches for these items include using standardised products, monitoring and/or optimising order volume, and optimising inventory levels.

[34] Kraljic, P. (1983) 'Purchasing Must Become Supply Management' *Harvard Business Review*.

that can determine the level of competition within an industry that can influence the respective bargaining power of employer and provider.

Consequently, before proceeding to subsequent stages, for the more significant packages, it makes sense for the project manager to have some indication from the sponsor and other key stakeholders regarding:

- the acceptability of different contracting strategies in terms of, for example: special purpose vehicles (SPVs), joint ventures, consortia, public private partnerships, design, build, operate contracts, types of alliance, capital or leased services, etc.;
- their appetite for different approaches, and why. Do they actually understand why they want a certain approach? – often they do not; and
- how the provider for each package will be selected in terms of selection process and selection criteria.

Putting the Kraljic and Bensaou models together, we might identify a conflict. For instance, the employer might decide, using Kraljic's model, that they want a balanced strategic arrangement. However, using Bensaou's model, they realise that the typical provider is much larger than them so the package would be, relatively, a much smaller investment for the provider. Consequently, from the provider's perspective, it will not necessarily be a strategic relationship and the commercial power, once a contract is entered into, would reside with the provider. As a result, the employer may decide to court *smaller* potential provider organisations to encourage them to bid, etc.

3. The complexity and the risk level of the work forming the package versus the expected lifetime of the relationship. Figure 3.8 illustrates how the correlation of the nature of the employer–provider relationship should be adapted depending on project complexity and duration.

- If at one extreme, you are buying a one-off commodity, for which there are multiple suppliers, then your procurement strategy for that package might well be to select on the basis of technical compliance and cheapest price using a 'transactional' contract.
- If it is a commodity in limited supply or is a standard service and for which there is a repeat demand, then you may wish to have a 'call-off' contract with some specific conditions to ensure constancy of supply. An appropriate contract with that provider may already be in place for your organisation.

Buyer–supplier relationships: Prior study has pointed out that the level of investment required to be made by the buyer and supplier can be a major factor in understanding the likely buyer–supplier relationship.

	Low	High
High (Buyer's specific investments)	Captive buyer	Strategic partnership
Low (Buyer's specific investments)	Market exchange	Captive supplier

Supplier's specific investments

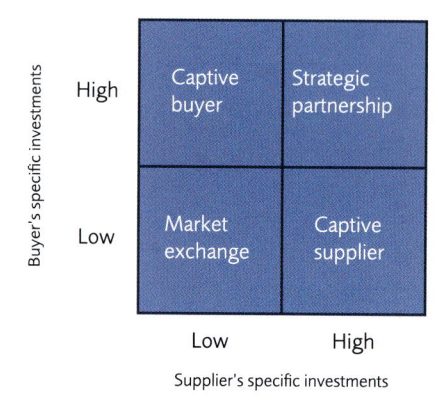

Figure 3.7 Buyer–supplier relationships (after Bensaou)

Based on buyer and supplier specific investments Bensaou identifies four types of buyer–supplier relationships:

Captive buyer: High buyer specific investments and low supplier specific investments. In this asymmetric relationship; the buyer is held hostage by a supplier that is free to switch to another customer.

Captive supplier: Low buyer specific investments and high supplier specific investments. This relationship is characterised by a supplier that enters the trap of unilaterally making idiosyncratic investments to win and keep the business with the customer.

Market exchange: Low buyer specific investments and low supplier specific investments. In this relationship neither of the parties has developed specialised assets to work with each other. Both parties can work together by using general-purpose assets. Both the buyer and the supplier can go to the market and shift to another partner at low cost and minimal damage.

Strategic partnership: High buyer specific investments and high supplier specific investments. In this partnership both parties put unusually high value assets into the relationship.

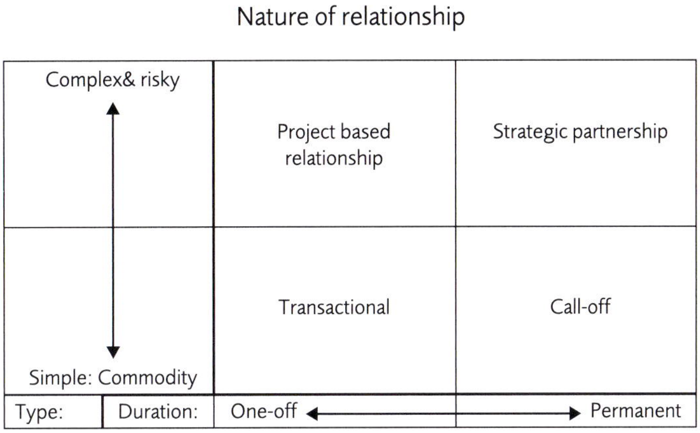

Project procurement strategy

Nature of relationship

		One-off ⟵	⟶ Permanent
Complex & risky ↕ Simple: Commodity		Project based relationship	Strategic partnership
		Transactional	Call-off
Type:	Duration:		

Figure 3.8 Correlating the nature of relationship with the project complexity and duration

- If you are letting a one-off works package, then you may require a 'project-based' relationship. The exact nature of the selection criteria and the contract will vary upon the complexity and risk and relative power of providers in that sector.
- It may be that your project is part of a programme of projects which have similar characteristics and key elements. In order to avoid repeating procurement costs, to encourage continuous improvement from project to project, or just to secure a scarce resource, you may decide that a strategic partnership needs to be put in place, using an appropriate form of agreement (e.g. teaming agreement, framework agreement). Note that a strategic partnership may also be considered for one-off endeavours if advantageous.

Although the employer will be the ultimate arbiter and risk holder for the overall endeavour, the more complex and risky a project is the more important it is to gain input from potential providers to fully understand the risks and complexity. The employer will define the preferred contracting strategy and hence the extent that the first order effects of risks are to be borne by each party. Providers have the choice of whether to accept the risk and complexity level or no-bid. In the case of strategic partnerships, which can often be longer term, the consultation between the parties may be more intensive; none-the-less the employer will still need to clearly define the ownership of delivery and risk clearly.

Consequently, before proceeding to subsequent stages, for the more significant packages, it makes sense for the project manager and team to have some indication from the sponsor and other key stakeholders regarding:

- the acceptability of each of the available contracting strategies as described in Chapter 4; taking into account the necessary commitment from the employer. For example the sponsor may prefer a fixed-price solution rather than an effort based one.
- how the provider for each package will be selected in terms of the selection process and the selection criteria used.

We recommend that the above factors are considered early on to avoid choosing a path which turns out to be unacceptable to the stakeholders and hence results in abortive detailed work and wasted time.

3.4 Outputs

For each significant package, there should be a procurement management plan outlining the overall approach taken and summarising:

- The package scope in terms of what is currently intended to be in that package. If there are any unusual, but deliberate, inclusions or omissions from the scope, they should be stated, together with the reasons for being included or omitted.
- A set of statements defining how the package interfaces with other packages or parallel work being done and any related dependencies. These statements should propose how these 'soft' boundaries will be managed.
- For packages that will be let externally under contract, a summary statement indicating what sort of contracting strategy and selection arrangements are acceptable (or unacceptable) to the project sponsor or steering group/project board. This can be directly derived from an analysis of the nature of the relationship sought.
- An outline budget for the provider selection process.
- For significant and/or complex endeavours a further output should be in the form of a benefits realisation plan document.

The less significant packages need to be categorised by type and by defining which procurement management method will apply. For instance, all goods may be managed in a similar way under similar selection and contracting strategies.

The procurement management plan should be signed-off by the project sponsor and, if appointed, the project board or steering group before proceeding to the next stage.

4

Package contracting strategy

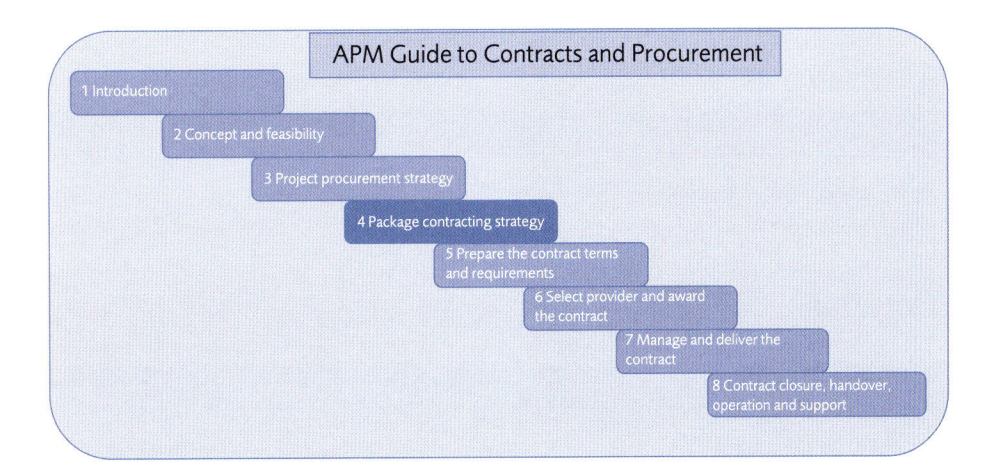

APM Guide to Contracts and Procurement
- 1 Introduction
- 2 Concept and feasibility
- 3 Project procurement strategy
- 4 Package contracting strategy
- 5 Prepare the contract terms and requirements
- 6 Select provider and award the contract
- 7 Manage and deliver the contract
- 8 Contract closure, handover, operation and support

4.0 Overview

This stage develops the contracting strategy for each individual package to be procured. During the stage, decisions are made on the main elements of the strategy for the providers of each of the packages. The strategy should include:

- The basis for how the provider is paid.
- The payment schedule (defining the cash flow).
- To whom risk is allocated and hence how it will be managed (allocated, contained and mitigated).
- How the parties are motivated, whether positively through bonuses and use of remedies in case of default.
- Choice of the contract terms, which may be based on a 'best fit' standard form of contract, or whether an in-house or custom form should be used.

The output from the stage will be a briefing document that will be used to instruct the drafting team for the contract terms and requirement (see Chapter 5).

APM Guide to Contracts and Procurement

4.1 Background

This stage is important because research within the construction industry[35, 36] has shown that contracting strategy has as large an effect on a contract's success as any technical decision. For instance, it is not unusual for contract strategy to demonstrably save 10 per cent on total costs to the employer on a single contract.[37] Some extreme examples have achieved up to 30 per cent cost savings.[38]

As discussed in section 1.1, the ability to influence the outcome of a project is highest during the early stages (see the Cost influence curve of Figure 1.4). This is also true for the process of developing the contract and choosing providers. If the drafting team is incorrectly briefed then there could be cost, time, and quality impacts due to the shortcomings of the final contract terms.

4.2 Risk management

At a high level, the contract strategy determines how the main risks associated with each contract package are allocated to the parties and the management practises to be used. The contract itself will allocate the risk, therefore the high level decisions should be made prior to the selection of any standard conditions of contract and before any subsequent drafting is done.

> **Risk event:** An uncertain event or set of circumstances that should it or they occur would have an effect on the achievement of one or more of the project objectives. *APM Body of Knowledge 6th edition*

A risk event can be categorised in two ways:

---

[35] Yates, A. (1991) 'Procurement and construction management' in P. Venmore-Rowland, P. Brandon and T. Mole (eds), *Investment, Procurement and Performance in Construction*, London: E. & F. N. Spon.
[36] Dhanushkodi, U. (2012) *Contract Strategy for Construction Projects*.
[37] Broom J. C. (2002) *Procurement Routes for Partnering: A Practical Guide*.
[38] For example, the Andrews Oilfield alliance in the North Sea. Source: Bakshi, A. (1995) 'Alliances Change Economics of Andrew Field Development', *Offshore Engineer*, 50(1).

- as a threat, which is a negative risk, which, if it occurs will have a detrimental effect on the project and/or risk holder; or
- as an opportunity, which is a positive risk, which, if it occurs will have a beneficial effect on the project and/or risk holder.

The Kraljic matrix (see section 3.3.6) may be used to consider how much of an effect a risk due to a particular employer–provider relationship would have on the overall project, and some of the strategies which might come out of this to manage it.

> **Risk owner:** The person who has responsibility for dealing with a particular risk on a project and for identifying and managing responses. *APM Body of Knowledge 6th edition*

The risk owner should not be confused with the entity having contractual liability. Although the entity having contractual liability will be an interested party, they may not be best placed to manage the risk itself. To avoid confusion, we define the risk holder as 'the organisation or organisations that are liable for the immediate consequences of the risk occurring, whether that liability leads to a positive or negative impact'. Notice that the term 'organisations' (plural) is used, as in collaborative relationships there may be a degree of risk sharing, which will need to be defined clearly in the final contract.

The term 'immediate consequence' is used, as there may be significant ramifications to the risk holder following a risk occurring. To take an extreme example: if liability for a risk event is allocated to a provider which is of such a magnitude that, if it occurs, it causes the provider organisation to go out of business, then ultimately that risk, together with all other risks allocated to that provider, will revert to the employer.

Risk is also an exposure of the project outcome itself, i.e. the ability of the package to be delivered. Some project risks may be secondary to the overall business/commercial risks faced due to an event. There is a danger that the project manager may be blinkered in considering the project itself, but will miss the overall business aims or miss an opportunity.

> **Project risk (risk):** The potential of an action or event to impact on the achievement of objectives. *APM Body of Knowledge 6th edition*

The overall 'variation in outcome' will be the sum of the impacts of the various risk events occurring, i.e. the risk events are the sources of variation, while the project impact is the consequence. We develop this to define contract risk as 'the contractual exposure of a party to the consequences (positive or negative) of variation in outcome resulting from the risk event and other uncertainties which they are allocated under the contract'.

The mechanism for risk allocation and sharing needs to be defined. For example, in a bi-party contract:

- A specific risk event may be shared subject to a threshold. For example, in civil engineering contracts, the provider typically takes the risk of adverse weather up to a defined threshold and should therefore allow some contingency in their contract prices. Beyond that threshold, the employer takes the additional risk.
- Contract risk may be shared by, for example, an overall pain/gain share mechanism. If costs come in above or below a contractual stated target figure the over or under run is shared to a pre-agreed formula.

It is worthwhile considering some principles of risk allocation and sharing, as they affect virtually all aspects of this chapter.

When allocating or sharing risk the following should be considered, in order:

1. **If the risk occurs, what will be the effect on the organisation's business?** If a threat is completely allocated to the provider, it will bear all the pain of any impact. In practice, however, some risk contingency would have been added to the contract price.

    The level of contingency may depend on the market: in a buoyant market, the provider might add in a large risk contingency to their contract price risk, which may not represent good value for money to the employer. However, in a depressed market where the provider is more desperate for work, the cost of risk transfer may well represent good value.

    In addition, if the potential cost of the risk's impact is high relative to the size of the contracted organisation, then a higher premium may need to be added, compared with a larger organisation, as the impact could be more significant to the individual business. This is why we use insurance: high impact, but unlikely risks are transferred to an organisation that can bear them.

    Also, if the contingency does not cover the impact cost then the contracted party may respond by being defensive, devoting energy trying to transfer contractual liability back to the employer at the expense of delivery.

In extreme cases, bankruptcy could follow and impacts will revert up the contractual chain to the employer. On the other hand, if none of the risk events allocated to the provider occur, then any reserved contingency becomes profit.

Example of the effect: In the construction industry, main contractors typically make 2 per cent profit on turnover. So a 1 per cent increase in their costs halves their profit. Consequently, with price-based contracts, they may fight tooth and nail to demonstrate that the employer in some way caused this increase through a related breach(es) of contract and is therefore liable. To the employer, they are arguing over peanuts – less than 1 per cent of the total contract costs – but for the provider it is 50 per cent of what matters to them i.e. their profit.

2. **Who can best influence the risk outcome?** Prevention is always better than cure. This should be a key working principle, but it also applies to who can best manage opportunity. Good management practice should maximise the potential for opportunities that reduce cost or time and maximise value; and minimise the opposites. All other things being equal – which in practice they rarely are – allocation of liability for a risk event should be to the party that can best proactively manage it.
3. **For a threat, which party is best placed to minimise any negative consequences (impacts)?** Allocating a risk to the party best able to minimise the consequences will motivate them to do so, and it avoids the temptation to make the most of the other parties' misfortune.
4. **Which party is best placed to own the minor risks?** For minor risks, all other things being equal, the parties may be relatively indifferent over responsibility. However, if a minor risk is likely to occur frequently and it is allocated to the employer, the consequence may be frequent arguments over minor adjustments to the contract prices and associated inefficiency. To avoid this, it is normally best to allocate such risks to the provider.

The above guidance points (1–4) are principles; in the real world, there may well be contradictions. For example:

- A small specialist software services company may be best placed to manage the risk associated with a critical part of a large organisation's IT system (due to their specialist knowledge), but may be unable to take the consequences of failure (impact costs and potential liquidated damages). In these circumstances, it is best to hold an open discussion; leading to an appropriate allocation of risk and hence adjustments to pricings, while still maintaining the provider's commercial motivation to succeed.

- A medium sized contractor working in a large live chemical facility – say doing some welding – is best placed to manage the risk of damage to the chemical works, but would very quickly become bankrupt if they caused a fire to the facility due to the costs of replacing the facility and the loss of revenue. A discussion around insurance cover, excesses, caps on liability, as well as appropriate oversite, will mean that the contractor is willing to take on the work without (a) adding an excessive risk premium and (b) going bankrupt.

4.3 Inputs

The inputs to this stage are the outputs from the previous stage (the project procurement strategy stage), which are used as the starting point for the development of the contracting strategy for each contract package or grouping of packages by type.

To recap, the outputs from the previous stage will be provided in the procurement management plan, which, as well as giving the overall procurement philosophy and approach for the whole project, includes for each package:

- The package scope.
- The package interfaces and dependencies with other packages and proposed guidance for their management.
- The nature of relationship sought with the provider.
- An outline budget for the provider selection process.

The latter nature of relationship is primarily what is developed in the package contracting strategy stage.

4.4 Activities

There are six key activities or sub-process steps within the package contracting strategy stage as illustrated in Figure 4.1 and which are described in this section.

Package contracting strategy

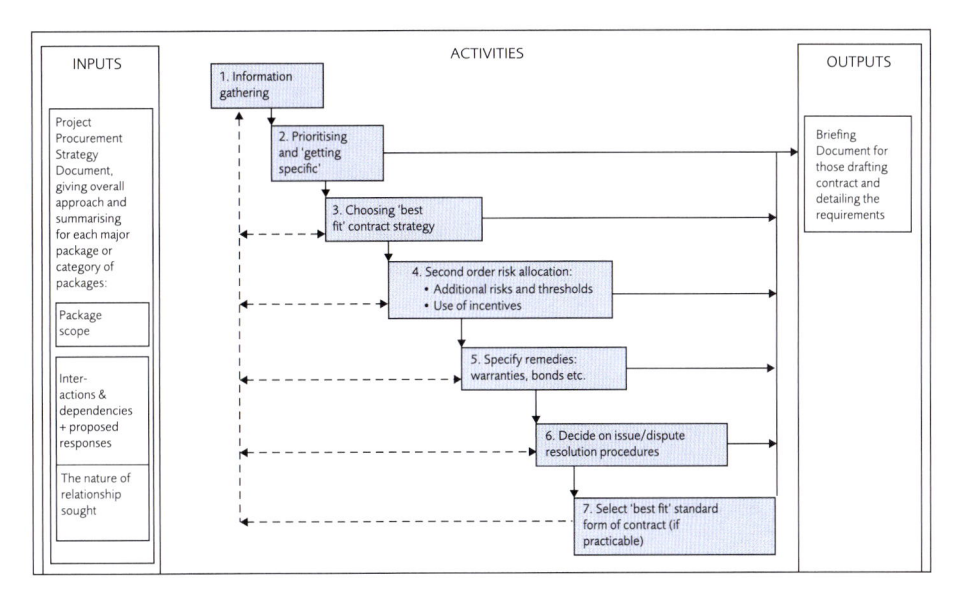

Figure 4.1 Process diagram for the package contract strategy stage

4.4.1 Activity 1: Information gathering

This stage is predominantly about gathering more detailed information regarding the package and the likely participants within it. This information is equally valuable for consideration in Stage 5 when selecting the provider. Information can be gathered under three inter-related main headings as below:

1. ***The participants' drivers and constraints:*** The employer needs to be clear about its drivers for the contract, as opposed to the project. For instance, the overall project may be time-driven, but the individual package may not be on the critical path of the overall project.

    Additionally, the employer's attitude to risk needs to be a consideration. For example, there may be an overarching desire for certainty (for example when completion dates are widely publicised). In this case the impact is unrelated to the employer's ability to absorb the direct consequences in terms of cost and time. The public sector, for example, may often have a mentality to be very risk averse (due to publicity), yet very few organisations have a greater ability to bear financial risk than a national government.

    The driving factors for the likely provider participants also need to be considered. It is all too easy to say that the commercial sector is only driven by money, or more precisely, profit only. Whilst this is partly true, it is often a simplification as other factors may also apply, for example how essential is it for them to:

- Be cash flow positive.
- Have continuity of work to preserve workforce and gain a consistent return on capital.
- Increase market share.
- Be willing to sacrifice some short-term profit from the contract in order to have a long-term profit stream from an employer.
- Have the certainty of profit versus the opportunity to maximise profit if the contract goes well; the opposite of which is making a loss if it does not. This can be reflected in the willingness to take contractual ownership of risk. In boom times, this may result in the cost for an employer to transfer a risk to a provider being inflated and vice versa in recessionary times.
- Just be able to get on with doing work that they are good at. This is true for many smaller specialist organisations. Consequently, they only do work for or give good prices to clients who they have a good working relationship with. In practice, this means a lack of administrative 'hassle' and being paid promptly and fairly for both original and additional work. Complex and time absorbing selection processes and sophisticated contracts do not play to their strengths.

Constraints also need to be identified. For instance, in government contracts, the need to be accountable and auditable strongly constrains how they can act, not just in documented written rules and procedures, but culturally as well. An overarching requirement to be cash flow neutral – in terms of funding and expenditure – is another common constraint.

Both *Drivers* and *Constraints* can take several forms. A useful high-level aide memoire is the acronym 'PESTLE', which stands for:

- **P**olitical: e.g. the political imperative to use a UK provider.
- **E**conomic: e.g. the need for an even spend in successive financial years.
- **S**ociological: e.g. the need to ensure local sub-suppliers or labour is used.
- **T**echnological: e.g. on a large project, there may be a need for common IT platforms amongst all providers for maintenance and management reasons.
- **L**egal: e.g. in the construction industry, construction contracts may have to comply with Acts of Parliament regarding payment and dispute resolution procedures.

- **E**nvironmental: e.g. the need to comply with environmental constraints in a planning application.

2. Strengths and weaknesses of the likely parties: Principally applying to:

- The parties' commercial ability to bear financial risk. For instance, a £250,000 risk might be a relatively minor risk to a £1bn turnover company, yet would potentially bankrupt a £1m turnover company. The former company might price the risk competitively and as a 'statistic' (like an insurance company); whereas the latter would need to price it higher in absolute terms as, relative to their size, it is a large risk and would be likely to cost more if insured against. Some entrepreneurial smaller organisations may be willing to take on a high level of risk, however this would increase the employer's risk due to the higher potential for provider bankruptcy.
- The parties' commercial and technical ability to manage different types of risk. See section 4.2 'Risk management aspects'.

3. Contract specific factors: A set of opportunities, threats, strengths and weaknesses may also apply due to the nature of the contract to be let.

These may have already been identified as high-level generic risks but need to be developed down to more tangible contract level risks. For instance, in a construction project, unforeseen ground conditions may have been identified as a generic project level risk. To gain greater certainty, however, further investigation (e.g. a geotechnical survey) might reveal more detail about the location and type of ground risk and consequences of occurrence, which in practice should lead to a smaller premium being placed on the risk, to everyone's real benefit.

Alternatively, there may be specific risks related to type of contract and/or its interaction with other parallel contracts. The PESTLE acronym (see above) may be used to identify sources of risk against which formal risk management techniques can be applied prior to entering into the contract.

4.4.2 Activity 2: Prioritising and getting specific

From the potentially large mass of information generated in Activity 1, it is necessary to pick out the key drivers and constraints, pertinent strengths, weaknesses and main risks in order to prioritise them, in terms of importance and address them in the form of contract. The question to be answered is: Of all the drivers determined via the various stakeholders, which are the key ones for a particular contract and how can they be expressed precisely in a contract?

The objectives of the package need to be identified as well as the points of leverage on the providers in negotiation and during delivery.

Where constraints are identified, they can be challenged and potentially made broader by asking two simple questions:

- 'Where does this constraint originate and what is the authority that governs the constraint requirement?' This identifies the cause; and
- 'What would happen if we did not have this constraint?' This identifies the consequences.

Generally, the fewer the constraints or restrictions on how the provider may deliver the contract, the more leeway there is for innovation. As a result of this, the important and real constraints should be left in, while the less important ones can be relaxed, re-expressed or removed.

Taking all the risks identified, it is essential to identify which are the main risks, to whom they are allocated both in terms of management and liability, as described in section 4.2 above, and how precisely they are to be expressed and allocated in the contract.

It may be argued that precisely defining objectives, constraints and risks at this stage is unnecessarily detailed or overbearing. However, without this precision, there are the risks that:

(a) Stakeholders and the project team may think they agree, while the reality is that they do not as they do not understand properly what they are alleged to agree, and
(b) Lawyers and technical people who will ultimately draft the contract and detail the requirements may define them incorrectly.

4.4.3 Activity 3: Choose 'best-fit' contracting strategy

Choosing the 'best fit' contracting strategy is about selecting the most appropriate 'big picture' risk allocation given the scope of the works in the future contract, the contract objectives, constraints, risks and the strengths and weaknesses of the likely parties to the contract.

The choice of contracting strategy may well have a significant bearing on the budget for the provider selection process, i.e. it may point to adjustment of the outline budget indicated as an input to this stage. Should the selection budget need adjustment then this should be subject to due governance and be agreed with the project sponsor. The outline budget (whether adjusted or not) will form an output from this stage.

The most commonly used contractual arrangements are listed below and individually described in the following paragraphs. We have attempted to identify the key features of each, how terminology might vary from industry or sector to sector and when to use them. It should be noted that those listed are 'archetypes' in that the contractual relationship will look 'something like' what is described, but may not necessarily conform precisely:

- Schedule of rates.
- Bill of quantities.
- Fixed price contract.
- Input-based arrangements: fee-based arrangements, management contracts and cost reimbursable contracts.
- Partnering/collaborative contracts: target cost contracts and project alliances.
- Strategic alliances: framework, strategic outsourcing and some joint ventures (JVs).
- Build, own, operate, transfer (BOOT)/design, build, finance and operate (DBFO) arrangements, including private finance initiatives (PFI)/public private partnerships (PPP).

Figure 4.2 correlates the most likely 'best fit' collaboration strategy against the complexity and/or timescale expected for the contract.

Schedule of rates

A schedule of rates is an arrangement in which the employer puts together a list of pre-identified goods or services, possibly with quantities against each item, and asks potential providers to tender against these rates. During contract execution, quantities of goods or labour hours are called off and the successful provider is paid against the quantities multiplied by the agreed rates.

A schedule of rates is typically used where the employer can define what they want, but not necessarily the quantity wanted or when they want it. Often, this arrangement is used for 'commodity-type' goods or services where there are multiple providers available. Consequently, the employer achieves value for money due to open competition, with a provider being chosen predominantly on the lowest total price for a combination of goods or services.

What sort of contracting strategy?

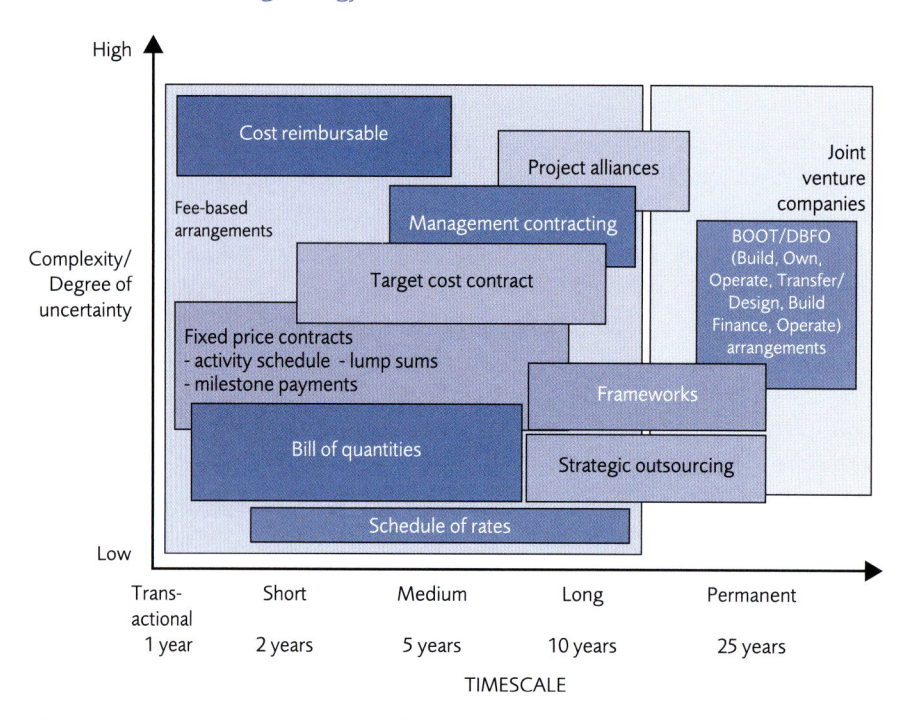

Figure 4.2 Most appropriate collaboration strategy against contract complexity/timescale

A schedule of rates can also be used in a longer term call-off contract, perhaps with multiple providers, whereby for any given order the employer evaluates which provider will give the best deal and places the order accordingly. Inflation and other factors affecting costs over time may need to be factored into the rates over the contract term.

A common misuse of a schedule of rates is where goods and services are required for the delivery of a series of individually unique projects, albeit in a similar market domain, with the intention that standard rates are used to build up the price for each project. In this context, the project may be delivered as an instructed task under a term contract or an individual contract under a framework agreement. The misuse arises due to trying to use standard 'model' rates which were tendered for circumstances which do not match those under which a package is delivered. Consequently, either prior to the contract or during the contract, the provider argues that the rates do not apply to the work being done.

Bill of quantities

A bill of quantities is very like a schedule of rates with the key difference being that, while the end requirement is defined, the quantity of work required to deliver the requirements is difficult to forecast accurately. The bill of quantities therefore 'provides project specific measured quantities of the items of work identified by the drawings and specifications in the tender documentation' but is subject to re-measure. The provider is therefore paid for the quantity of work they do as the contract progresses as opposed to that called-off by the employer. For instance, in civil engineering, the bill of quantities, upon which the provider tenders, is an estimate of, for instance, the volumes of earth, by type, that needs to be moved. The volume moved is measured once the work has been done, with the provider being paid a tendered rate multiplied by the quantity of work done.

A problem with this approach is that the costs to the provider of doing the work are not solely related to the quantities involved. Other factors may have a significant effect. In the earthworks example, the ground type found and the prevailing weather conditions can have major effects on the provider's programme and hence time-related costs. If the bill of quantity rates do not sufficiently cover these indirect costs, then argument may result during package delivery. Consequently, the tendered rate per unit is often subject to change.

Fixed price contracts

Fixed price contracts are a generic category of contracts based on the establishment of firm legal commitments to complete the required work. A performing provider is legally obligated to finish the job, no matter how much it costs to complete, for the amount that they have tendered. Selecting a technically competent and financially secure provider should give the employer a high degree of certainty of outcome. Consequently, these arrangements should be used only where the employer can clearly describe:

- What it is they want. This need not necessarily be fully detailed as the provider is usually best able to do this, but sufficiently and unambiguously defined so that the employer will get the outputs, and hence outcomes, they want.
- The constraints under which it is delivered.
- Where the risks, from the provider's perspective, are relatively small and quantifiable, i.e. a 'strength' of theirs is doing work of this sort, so it is low risk

because of their expertise and experience. These arrangements are normally used where the contract is to deliver a full package.

If fixed price contracts are used when a significant degree of change is likely, there will be added risks to contend with, as:

- Providers may inflate the costs attributed to changes to reclaim any lost profit that they may have incurred (or to increase overall profit). It is almost always costlier to change provider mid-stream than to put up with inflated costs against changes.
- Providers may argue that because they were so keenly priced at the bid stage with all activities planned in detail any changes will cause delay and disruption costs. And they may well be telling the truth.

Thus, where the requirement is uncertain and subject to change or the employer does not meet their side of the contractual bargain, a fixed price contract can end up as anything but a fixed price.

Similarly, the allocation of ownership of risk is an important consideration for fixed price contracts. If the employer retains a large proportion of the risk in the form of dependencies, then significant cost may be incurred should the risk become a reality. However, if significant risk is transferred to the provider, then the employer may well pay an inflated risk premium in the initial contract price. Consequently, where fixed price contracts are used for complex projects, the provider needs to be vetted to ensure that it can cost-effectively manage the risks allocated. The choice of a suitably skilled provider is therefore paramount.

There are several variants on fixed price contracts in terms of how the provider is paid:

- *Milestone payments* when typically the employer has described deliverables in a milestone payment plan. For less complex contracts this can be quite straightforward and a useful system to focus both parties on the progress to be made under the contract. However, there are circumstances where the effect is not benign. For instance:
  - The provider may front-load the milestone payments to gain positive cash flow and minimise his ongoing risk, to the detriment of the employer.
  - There may be little transparency of costs associated with changes, especially if the payment milestones are defined at a high level and do not correlate

directly with the programme tasks. The provider then takes advantage of this lack of transparency when change occurs.
- *Lump sums* where the provider breaks the works down into discrete operations and is paid at regular intervals according to percentage completion of each task or operation. This can provide more transparency of cost than milestone payments as the lump sum payments can more closely match the programme progress. It is important to describe each operation at an appropriate level, as if each operation is described at too high a level there may be arguments over the percentage of work completed. Earned value analysis can be a useful tool in assessment with this method. However, the related tasks will still need to be described at an appropriate level of detail.
- *Activity schedules* (which may be referred to as 'milestones' in the IT sector, causing some confusion in definition) are like lump sums except that the provider is only paid against completed 'activities'. Consequently, in this system the providers are required to break their activity schedule down to a more granular level than is normally the case with lump sums. This can be advantageous in providing greater transparency and easier monitoring. The disadvantage is, however, usually the need for more work at the tendering stage for the providers.

As fixed price contracts are often tendered against functional or performance specifications, the potential providers are likely to have to do some design or developmental work at the pre-contract stage to derive a price to tender. Employers will need to check the output of this work to ensure that it meets with their requirement. The resulting design must then be incorporated into the contract. One of the key things to ensure is that the provider's design must satisfy the employer's requirement rather than, in the case of ambiguity or inconsistency, over-write it. Consequently, the contract must state, either directly or indirectly, that the employer's requirement has 'precedence' over the provider's design.

Depending on the type of project, doing the design or developmental work to a level where a meaningful price can be tendered can be quite onerous on the tendering providers. Consequently, some employers may initially ask for outline designs and indicative prices. They then select the best submission via a down-select process and work with the preferred provider to de-risk the contract package and develop the design to give the employer sufficient certainty of what will physically be delivered. As a result, the provider can price more accurately and the employer should have a more sharply priced contract to enter into. This is called a 'preferred provider' route.

Unfortunately, once a preferred provider is chosen, even though the employer has the option of going to another provider, as time progresses the employer becomes increasingly tied into using this provider and this can open up the relationship to exploitation by the provider. Consequently, this approach is usually used by repeat order employers holding a controlled group of favoured providers, where there is the incentive of a longer term overarching commercial relationship.

Turnkey contracts: A turnkey contract is usually let as a fixed price contract and is a comprehensive contract in which the provider is responsible for the supply of a completed facility, usually with responsibility for fitness for purpose, training operators, pre-commissioning and commissioning. It usually has a fixed completion date, a fixed price and guaranteed performance levels. Once complete, the employer 'turns the key' to make it work.

Input-based arrangements

Input-based arrangements are where the provider's costs are reimbursed plus an allowance for overheads and profit. They therefore rely on trust between the parties to operate effectively. There are three main input-based arrangements:

1) *Fee based arrangements*: whereby the provider provides gives their fee per unit of time at the start of the arrangement. Within some agreed constraints, such as demonstrating that time charged was spent on the employer's project, payment is based on the quantity of time used multiplied by the rates. This arrangement is often used at the start of a project where any poor decisions made or work done up-front can have a large effect later on. Consequently, it is seldom worthwhile skimping on this early stage. Having said this, many professional appointments are also made on this basis for the management of projects, e.g. in construction management a provider is appointed as a professional to manage the construction works with all the works contracts being made directly with the employer often on a fixed price or bill of quantities basis. This does, however, call for strong project leadership from the employer. In the IT sector this role is sometimes referred to as that of the 'integrator'.

2) *Cost reimbursable contracts*: whereby the provider does the work at cost, which could include management costs and, provided it can be evidenced

that these costs were incurred in providing the asset or service, payment is made of cost plus a tendered uplift fee. To be reimbursed the provider has to be able to provide evidence of his costs (via receipts, timesheets, accounts etc.) thus supplying a level of cost transparency. The uplift may be a fixed fee, or a percentage fee applied to the costs incurred. This arrangement tends to be used where there is an existing commercial relationship and time-driven or quality-driven work emerges, often carrying significant risk. For instance, in emergency work, it avoids the need for the requirement to be fully developed and then priced by the provider, including allowances for unknown or unquantifiable risk. Instead, the appointment can be made quickly and work started almost immediately.

3) *Management based contracts*: whereby the main provider only manages the work, as in the case of a construction manager or an integrator. However, the management contractor (provider) does not carry out any physical work, but manages the project for a fee, which is paid on top of the construction costs incurred by the management contractor. The management contractor then employs and pays works contractors to carry out the actual works. In effect, management contracting consists of 100 per cent subcontracting. This gives a 'harder' contract as the management-based provider has a 'fitness for purpose' liability to deliver, as opposed to a 'reasonable skill and care' liability and liquidated damages may be levied for late delivery. The downside is that the requirement must be more extensively developed to define the 'fit for purpose' liability and a 'hard' delivery date must be established. As the provider takes on commercial liabilities, it potentially has a position to defend, which may undermine the professional incentive to work in the best interests of the employer. For instance, if the project is running late, there is an incentive to spend the employer's money to avoid late delivery damages. Equally, if the employer introduces a change, there is a potential motivation to exaggerate the amount of additional time needed to cover up for other delays for which the provider would pay damages.

The main drawback of such arrangements is the lack of a direct contractual incentive to reduce costs. It was mainly for this reason that partnering/collaborative arrangements evolved.

Partnering/collaborative arrangements

Partnering is defined as an arrangement between two or more organisations to manage a contract between them cooperatively (as distinct from a legally established 'partnership'). At the time of writing, 'partnering' has fallen out of fashion and 'collaboration/collaborative working' is in. The difference seems to be a realisation that delivering to the contract, both in what is physically delivered and the rigour with which good contract and project management is applied, is important. Consequently, contracts are written to be more user friendly so that people can follow, as opposed to ignore, what the contracts say.

While partnering and collaborative working can be done under any of the previously mentioned contracting strategies, certain strategies lend themselves to this approach due to the way in which they provide cost transparency and align commercial objectives.

Under partnering arrangements, the primary means of reimbursing the provider is through direct payment of their costs, plus an uplift fee to cover overheads and profit as per cost reimbursable contracts above. The parties can then work on taking out cost towards a contractually meaningful savings target (see target cost contracts below). Adjustments to this target can be agreed when employer-held risk events occur.

The commercial alignment comes from a meaningful target being established; around which savings and overruns of cost-plus-fee are shared. This is often referred to as a pain/gain share mechanism and creates the incentive for both parties to work together to minimise costs. Essentially this means that there needs to be sufficient scope within the technical requirement to take out cost, either through managing out threat or managing in opportunity via collaborative working. There is little point in using this type of contract for a fully defined and detailed requirement in which the employer is not going to contribute.

There are several types of contracting arrangements which reflect the scope for cooperation, innovation and joint risk management as described in the following paragraphs.

Target cost contracts: Are formed between two parties, where a contract target price is tendered, negotiated or built up on an open book basis. This target essentially comprises the provider's costs, an allowance for the risks included within the target and the necessary uplift fee. The pain/gain share operates around this target.

During the contract, the target is adjusted for pre-defined reasons, normally to do with the employer changing something, not doing something which they are contractually obligated to do (which would otherwise be a breach of contract) or a limited number of third party events over which the provider has no control.

Package contracting strategy

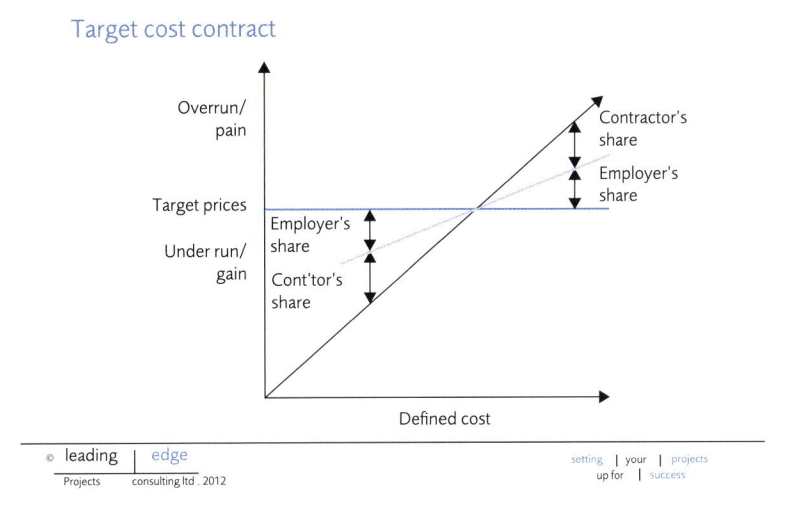

Figure 4.3 A target cost contract with approximately 50:50 share of any over and under run compared with the target prices

A specific type of target cost contract is the *guaranteed maximum price (GMP) contract*. The essential difference is that at some point, often the target, the employer's share of any overrun is capped, so that the provider takes all the pain beyond this point. In addition, the allowable reasons for adjusting the agreed target may often be specified according to the legal minimum.

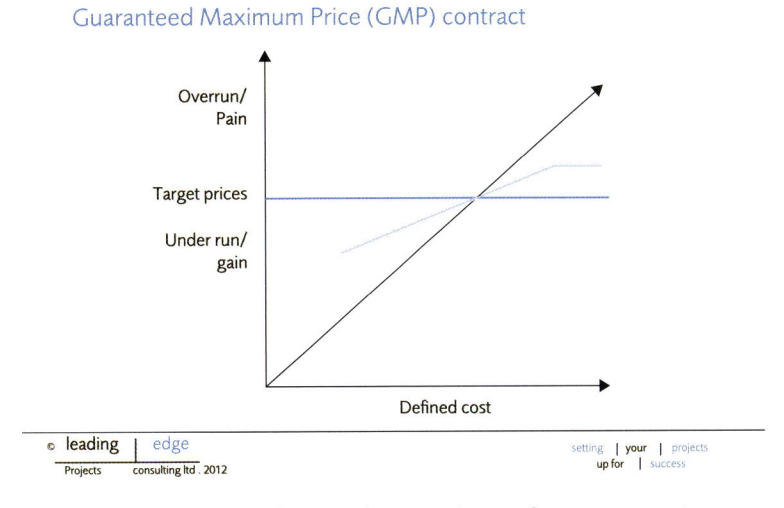

Figure 4.4 Illustrating that the employer's share of any overrun is capped at approximately 10 per cent overrun on the target prices

Project alliances

Project alliances typically have the following characteristics compared with target cost contracts:

- There are more than two parties tied into the alliance incentive mechanism, i.e. the employer and several key providers.
- There is usually a 'courting' phase where the parties work together on a fee basis to develop a sufficiently robust requirement and the alliance contact price target, which is agreeable between the parties. This has parallels with the preferred provider route discussed above. Note, however, that if the requirement is over-developed it can defeat the objective of entering an alliance.
- The alliance target price is normally quite extensive in its coverage, including budget for almost all risks normally borne by the employer, as well as other project related costs, e.g. management costs and (in construction) land-take, etc. Note that the costs of external audit are usually excluded from the alliance costs.
- Because of the previous two points, the reasons for any adjustment to the alliance target price are far fewer than under a target cost contract.

Alliances are used where there are significant interdependencies, not just between the employer and each provider, but also between the providers. Such interdependencies can be a cause of significant negative risk/threat, but also may present significant opportunity. Rather than trying to manage interdependencies in a top-down way, due to the alignment of motivations to the success of the project, the parties work together in a more egalitarian way to solve issues and risks for mutual benefit.

Early provider involvement – called Early Contractor Involvement (ECI) in construction – is a half-way house between the target cost contract approach and a full project alliance. Here the provider works at cost with the employer to develop the requirement to a point where it can be priced. At this point a target cost contract is entered into; but with the provider typically taking responsibility for the developed design. In other words, under a target cost contract, if there is an error in the requirement, the employer corrects it and the target cost is adjusted. Under ECI, the cost of any error is included within the target cost, thus creating greater commercial alignment.

Prime contracting is similar to the Early Provider Involvement route with two further developments:

Package contracting strategy

- A greater emphasis on collaborative working for the parties involved down the supply chain, with them being incentivised accordingly.
- A fitness-for-purpose liability for design as well as materials and workmanship, such that whilst the provider is paid on an open book basis with pain/gain share, its liabilities for the resulting solution are closer to those of the turnkey contract model.

Strategic alliances

Strategic alliances generally take two main forms:

1) *Project based frameworks;* whereby an employer enters a framework agreement or contract to use a provider, or group of providers, for projects of a certain type over a period of time. In practice, almost all such agreements will have a non-exclusivity clause whereby the employer is not obliged to use the provider. Indeed, most employers keep their options open by having several providers in any framework agreement. This is to both promote some competition and to avoid becoming dependent on just one provider. While the early projects under such an arrangement may be defined enough to price easily, later ones may need more extensive development before a meaningful price can be agreed. As each package requirement matures, an associated contract is let. Often, the contract is in the form of one of the previous partnering-style arrangements, i.e. target cost or alliance.

    Project based frameworks have the following advantages: they avoid the need to continually go out to the market; they reduce the need for a provider to do full tenders on a speculative basis, thus reducing overhead; they allow the provider to make longer-term investments as there is a greater likelihood of future work; and, if planned intelligently, they can allow for continuity of use of resources as opposed to de-mobilising and re-mobilising. Additionally, they can allow for continuous improvements to be made, as lessons learnt from one project can be taken account of in subsequent ones and this continuous improvement also includes team working. Such continuous improvement can result in progressive and sustained improvements in project delivery in terms of time, cost and quality.

    A potential downside is the danger of complacency creeping into a relationship, especially where a single provider is used for all the work. Consequently, most employers select several framework providers for a specific type of work and benchmark performance, rewarding the better performing ones with a greater share of the work.

APM Guide to Contracts and Procurement

2) Term service or *strategic outsourcing arrangements;* whereby a level of service is stated as a requirement, for example the maintenance of an asset, e.g. a road or building or for an IT-based service. The project could be delivered under a schedule of rates or fixed price contract, with performance falling below an agreed level being a reason for termination. What makes this a strategic alliance is:
- Whatever the service is, it is normally described in terms of a performance and/or functional requirement; in order to allow for continuous improvement, with both parties being able to contribute to improvements.
- The nature of the service operated tends to be strategic or business-critical to the employer organisation.
- The improvements can be in terms of cost-savings, which are shared by a pain/gain formula and/or in measures around the quality of service against which incentive payments are paid.

Joint venture

A *joint venture (JV)* is a contractual arrangement in which resources are combined, be they equipment, expertise or finance, by two or more participants with a view to carrying out a common purpose. This typically takes one of the following forms:

- A consortium agreement.
- A limited liability company.
- A partnership.
- A limited liability partnership (whereby the partners' liability is limited).

A subtlety can be whether it is:

- A vertical joint venture; for instance, a Local Authority and term services provider would normally be in a more traditional employer/provider arrangement. Instead, they could form a joint venture to both carry out this work and seek out extra work within that region for other clients. The profits could then be split per their respective ownership of shares.
- A horizontal joint venture; whereby two or more parties come together to jointly pursue and realise an opportunity which neither could pursue on their own.

Package contracting strategy

More specific reasons for forming a joint venture could include a combination of:

- Limitation of risk; whereby neither party could bear, or wish to bear, the entire consequences of the downside risk on their own.
- Pooling of resources, either because the opportunity is too big for only one party or because they have complementary expertise and neither party could deliver the opportunity without the other.
- Access to a market, particularly for work in overseas jurisdictions, where a foreign provider may have to form a joint venture with a local provider to qualify for access to the respective market.
- The advantage of a more integrated/efficient approach due to the elimination of contractual interfaces.

The main disadvantage of a joint venture approach is the significant cost and risk of setting one up, meaning that the size of the opportunity must be worth this cost. The setting-up costs not only include legal costs, but also those of defining the commercial reasons and scope of the arrangement, the strategic direction and management of it once established and the day-to-day integration of systems and cultures once it is place. There is therefore a significant risk that a joint venture may fail.

Often horizontal joint ventures are formed to enable the contractual approaches outlined below.

Build, operate, transfer (BOT) contracts where the employer has a requirement for something to be supplied to them and this requires a specialist facility to be built. For instance, the employer may require energy to be provided to a remote production facility close to the base resource. They therefore want a specialist energy company to take full responsibility for the building and operating of the asset but, after a set period, operation of the asset is transferred to the employer. Typically, this is paid for as a combination of a lump sum for setting up the facility and as a schedule of rates/bill of quantities for delivery of each unit of, in this instance, power.

Build, own, operate, transfer (BOOT) contracts are like BOT contracts except that the provider owns the facility for a set period, so the transfer is both of operations and ownership. The emphasis of payment shifts much more onto the delivery of the output as opposed to the build, i.e. the provider finances the build much more in return for larger payments per unit of output.

Design, build, finance and operate (DBFO) contracts (when the employer is the Public Sector, known as private finance initiative (PFI) or public private partnerships (PPP)): Such arrangements are similar to the BOOT arrangement above except, due to the size of the project and the duration of the operate phase, a financing organisation, such as a bank, needs to be part of the joint venture. Thus, often a special purpose vehicle – a new joint venture company – is created for the opportunity.

These contracts are usually associated with the design and implementation of a new or improved asset, service, or system. The 'build' part is derived from the original use for heavy engineering projects. Once the delivered asset is in operation, the employer pays the provider organisation(s) on its operation, often with a large part of this payment based on operational performance. For example, for a (non-toll) road, it may be based on the percentage of time that all lanes can be used and/or average traffic speed. These payments against operational performance both service and progressively pay off the providers' debt with an allowance for profit. The arrangement often includes a clause whereby, if performance slips below an agreed threshold for a given duration, the employer can take over ownership of the asset. Often, built into the contract is a requirement to upgrade the asset towards the end of the 'operate' phase before ownership reverts to the employer.

The typical contractual structure of such a PFI is shown in Figure 4.5.

The advantage of this approach is the focus of the contract on the ultimate performance achieved, the capability it gives the employer, and the benefits it delivers and within this broad frame, the allocation of risk to the party best able to manage it.

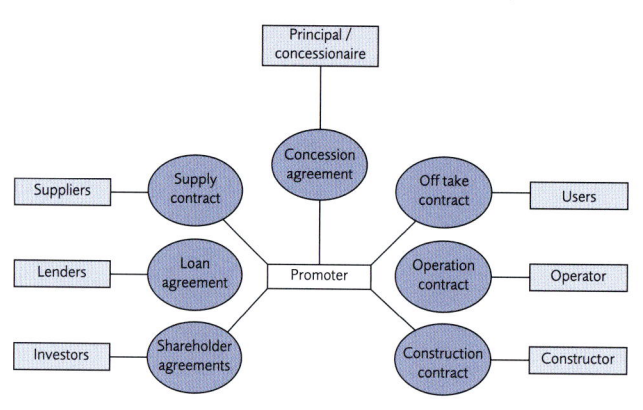

PFI : What does it look like contractually?

Figure 4.5 Example contractual structure of a PFI arrangement

There are essentially three types of PFI contract:

1) *Pure PFI*; which are normally commercially viable without financial support, sometimes identified and promoted by a concession company provider, e.g. the Channel Tunnel Rail Link.
2) *Part PFI*; which are not commercially viable on their own, thus 'sweeteners', such as ownership of existing assets are included in the contract. For instance, in the Second Severn Crossing, the first bridge was handed over to the concessionaire for them to derive income from, both during construction and afterwards.
3) *Public private partnerships*; where a government holds a competition, and selects a concession company provider to run a service on its behalf and pays the provider for doing it. These are not widely different from PFI projects, however they often function as outsourced services, where the quality of the outputs from the concession company provider are partially dependent on the inputs coming in from the government employer (i.e. there is greater interdependency between the two parties).

The main drawbacks of the DBFO, PFI and PPP approaches include:

- The cost of setting up such an arrangement, e.g. for a whole life cost of less than £25m it is unlikely for it to be worthwhile.
- The performance required, capability required or benefits wanted must be identified as tangible enough to be specified as a contractual requirement which can be measured and paid against.
- Howsoever the above criteria are expressed, they must be sufficiently long-lasting to be valid for the duration of the 'operate' term. For instance, the purpose of a road may well stay the same for a 25-year concession, but for a hospital, the purpose, range of functions and demand for them for that duration might vary enormously. Consequently, unforeseeable change can occur for which (a) the provider will want payment and (b) may mean the original criteria against which they are paid becomes invalid and/or untenable due to these changes.

4.4.4 Activity 4: Second order risk allocation

Having selected the primary risk allocation by choosing the 'best fit' contracting strategy, the next step is to fine tune the contracting strategy by deciding on:

- What risk events are excluded from the contract prices and would cause an adjustment to it. In some instances, this means defining thresholds for the risks above which they may invoke a contract change. For instance, in construction contracts, this could be the level of rainfall in a particular month.
- The degree to which the provider will be incentivised to meet the contractual level of performance and potentially exceed it.

4.4.4.1 Activity 4a: Additional risks and thresholds

Which risk events will cause an adjustment to the contractual sum should be precisely identified (to be precisely expressed in the subsequent contract) and allocated or shared in accordance with the principles identified in section 4.2 of this chapter.

Issues during contract delivery commonly arise due to the deletion (from standard forms) or non-inclusion of clauses that provide for adjustments due to breaches of contract by the employer or his representatives. Removing such clauses is generally pointless and should be very carefully considered before making any such amendment to the contract. The removal of such a mechanism potentially leads to the provider claiming 'breach of contract' and suing the employer for compensation, whether monetary or for offset against the penalties for delays incurred. It can lead to an extended delay to contractual completion sign-off and indeed the success of the overall project may become at risk. In addition to the resulting uncertainty, it may, in practice, become more expensive and time consuming than would be managing and agreeing contractual changes under the conditions of contract as the contract progresses.

It is far better to have the reasons for adjustment and the mechanism defined in the contract.

Linked to this, is the importance of having clauses which allow for changes in circumstances whilst the contract is being delivered, e.g. changes to the requirement whether in its scope or to upgrade its performance. Failure to have these provisions in the contract will either result in the provider refusing to do the work – and the asset potentially not being fit for purpose – or the provider being able to 'hold the employer to ransom' by re-negotiating the contract on their terms. During the contractual negotiations, therefore, discipline needs to be exercised to ensure that only essential changes are made to standard forms.

Lastly, third-party, or uncontrollable risk events for which the employer will take some or all of the risk need to be identified and defined. These fall into two camps:

1. Unlikely, but high impact risks: These should be allocated on the basis of whom can best bear the consequences, which will typically be the financially stronger party. An example is the risk of a third party's employees taking strike action, which eventually could have an impact on the time/cost/quality of the works being conducted.
2. Frequently occurring, but minor impact risks where the cumulative impact of them occurring can become significant. For instance, if a provider is working on a live asset such as a railway, where staff have to stop frequently for trains to pass with undefined frequency.

For the former, the risk transfer threshold may be set, for example, whereby the provider takes liability for the first week of any delay caused by the strike. For the latter, it may be decided that the provider takes the liability of 'X' stoppages of up to 'Y' minutes per month which is set a little above the normal amount to be expected. Above this point, the additional impact is allocated to the employer.

4.4.4.2 Activity 4b. Use of incentives

Incentives can be either set negatively in the form of liquidated damages or positively in the form of bonus or gain share. More often, only liquidated damages are specified. A prerequisite for the use of incentives is that the level of performance; be it in time-saving, efficiency improvements, service level improvement, cost-saving, etc., needs to be measurable and specified unambiguously. Another prerequisite is the use of common sense: achieving the desired level of performance has to be within the control of the party targeted by the incentive (i.e. benefitting or not according to the results). This is allied to the principles of risk allocation and sharing described in the overview of this chapter (section 4.2).

The most common trigger for liquidated damages is late delivery (delay damages). Liquidated damages may also be applied due to performance being below the level stated in the contract. For performance damages to apply, the performance requirement(s) have to be stated in a 'performance specification'. If the quantum of damages per unit time or unit of performance are not stated in the contract, then the employer may claim for the true cost, both direct and consequential, of this lack of attainment. This can lead to an expensive legal process and therefore some providers refuse to tender for work unless the performance requirement(s) and quantum of damages per unit of underperformance are stated. For this reason, it is normal practice to specify the maximum level of time related damages in the contract. For the majority of the world, with the notable exception of the USA and the Arab world, the maximum level of damages may not exceed a genuine pre-estimate of likely loss at the time that the contract comes into existence,[39] otherwise they can be legally challenged as a penalty.

The upshot of stating the maximum level of damages is to state the maximum liabilities which can fall on the contracting party, which reflects the parties' ability to bear risk and the premium the employer is willing to pay for risk transfer. Typical limitations on liabilities may include: maximum time related damages payable; maximum performance related damages payable; maximum liability for indirect or consequential loss; maximum liability for damage to an employer's property; maximum liability for design defects (if the provider is responsible for design); and maximum total liability.

A negative incentive also applies to those contracts where there is a 'pain share/gain share' mechanism for cost (pain), i.e. the provider may bear a share of the pain under a partnering style contract. While some employers choose to cap their own liability for any overrun through use of a guaranteed maximum price (GMP) contract, others choose to go the other way; whereby they cap or more often considerably reduce a provider's share of any large overrun. This typically happens on big contracts with a financially strong employer (relative to the provider), where the provider cannot bear the financial consequences of a contract that has gone significantly wrong.

The other side of the coin to damages are bonuses, which are generally paid for performance above the acceptable level stated in the contract or, less often, for meeting it, e.g. meeting the opening date of a venue which cannot slip. Obviously, it is only worthwhile specifying bonuses if the increase in performance is of benefit to the employer. Equally obvious, the employer does not give all the benefit to the provider as then none is left for themselves. However, incentives need to be set at a level that makes it worthwhile for the provider to pursue.

Bonuses are currently not used as much as are liquidated damages in the United Kingdom. Research[40] has found that a well thought out incentive plan stimulates superior contractual performance; whereas use of liquidated damages

---

[39] Note however, that in 2016, the English Supreme Court expanded the definition of what 'cost' is to include reputational and other hard to quantify impacts. In addition, the judgement downgraded the importance of this principle, especially in B2B contracts, relative to the parties' 'freedom to contract' on agreed terms. Consequently, the courts are even more reluctant to dismiss pre-stated damages as a penalty, unless they are judged 'extravagant, exorbitant or unconscionable'.
[40] CIPS (2014) *Supplier Incentivisation*.

alone has negligible or even detrimental effect on project performance. The psychology behind this is:

- It is always in both parties' interests to strive for bonus payments. Consequently, even when difficulties are encountered, people continue working together to try and achieve them.
- Whereas, when it becomes evident that the contractually defined level of performance is unlikely to be met, the provider may naturally try to put blame on the employer in order to avoid paying the damages (defensive behaviour). The employer, for similar reasons, then will try to put the blame back on the provider. This process can escalate instead of the parties working together to resolve the underlying cause of the lack of performance.

Our view is that it would be beneficial if incentives were used more widely to stimulate superior contractual performance. Furthermore, in complex situations with interdependent contractual obligations (when, for instance, there is a contract to deliver business-level benefits) it can be hard to show that the employer has no responsibility for the under-performance of the provider and consequently difficult to enforce liquidated damages.

Partnering style contracts may also be used to enable the sharing of gain. A note of caution though, as if these gains are made entirely through the efforts of the provider parties, without the collaboration of the employer – for instance under a target cost arrangement – then this mechanism may be viewed by the provider as a mechanism for reducing the provider's profit level solely for the benefit of the employer. Consequently, the provider may set the initial target cost at a higher level to adjust for this potential loss of profit.

4.4.5 Activity 5: Remedies

This section covers retentions, guaranties, warranties; as applicable for contracts in the United Kingdom including the need to allow for The Contracts (Rights of Third Parties) Act 1999. Essentially retentions, guaranties, warranties are remedies for under-performance of the provider against the performance requirement(s) where stated in the contract. Damages, as discussed in the previous Activity 4, can also be considered a remedy. Such means of redress may also be flowed-down to the subcontract level.

Retention is where payment is retained as the contract progresses (whether a proportion of each due stage payment or as a retention to be paid following completion of a warranty period) in order to ensure satisfactory performance or completion of contract terms. Typical levels may be 3 to 5 per cent of contract value (or stage payment values) although higher levels may also be specified. An arrangement may be that once the provider has completed the works, then a proportion – usually half – of any accumulated retention is paid back with the remainder following after a period in which the provider has a contractual obligation to correct defective works. Typically, this period is 12 months, though this depends upon the industry. The retention payment is paid minus any costs attributable to the provider for non-performance, e.g. where the employer has to correct any outstanding defects, which the provider should have corrected.

The purpose of retention payments therefore is to ensure that the provider completes the works; that it has minimal defects; that if there are any defects, the provider will correct them; and if not, the employer has some money to correct the defects themselves.

The downside of applying payment retention is that it detracts from the cash flow of the provider, causing it finance costs. Consequently, providers may include the financing cost in their contract price. As a result, particularly where there is an overarching repeat order commercial arrangement, some employers have stopped this practice and demand instead a form of bond. Bonds are often cheaper to finance and can take several forms, e.g. bid bond, advanced payment bond, performance bond and warranty bond. All, however, require the involvement of an extra party – a financial institution – which will charge for guaranteeing the corresponding payment covered by the bond.

Some employers (and providers flowing down retentions to subcontractors) have abused the retention system, by holding on to cash when not entitled to, which has caused the providers to price on the basis that they will not get retention back at all.

An additional drawback is that the sum retained after the works have been completed may not be enough to cover major defects in the work, leading to legal proceedings, which the implementation of the retention was intended to avoid.

Guarantees are legally enforceable assurances of the performance of a contract by a provider. Typically, a third party guarantees the performance of the provider under the contract. Should the provider not perform to the assigned level, or refuse to rectify their lack of performance, then the third party guarantees to pay for the associated costs up to a limit specified under the contract. An independent party is normally required to witness the signing of a guarantee for it be legally effective and (another) independent party is normally required to confirm any compliance or non-compliance and whether non-compliance is due to the provider.

The two most common forms of guarantee are:

- *Provider parent company guarantee*: The advantage of this to the provider is that the cost to take out this guarantee is likely to be minimal or non-existent compared with taking out a bond (see below). However, it is unlikely that the provider's parent company is independent either in mind-set or finances. Consequently, in a dispute over who is liable for the lack of performance, the guarantor is likely to listen to and take the side of the provider and be hesitant to pay out. Financially, if the provider defaults due to financial pressures from their parent company, e.g. it goes into administration, then the parent company is unlikely to be able to fulfil the guarantee.
- *A guarantee bond* from a bank or other financial institution: The advantage of this over the parent company guarantee is that a financial institution is assumed to be more independent and supposedly financially stronger (although following the banking crises of recent years, this was not the case). The disadvantage is that the provider has to pay for this bond and the cost is added onto the contract price which the employer will pay. More recently, financial institutions have limited the number of bonds they are prepared to issue to any organisation, in order to limit their exposure should that company cease to be in business.

A *warranty*, in this context, is a promise given by a provider to an employer regarding the nature, usefulness or condition of the supplies or services delivered under the contract, usually at a level set above that required under statutory law, with the remedy being liquidated damages payable. Two common forms are:

- A warrant for *fitness for purpose*: a provider of a service, under UK statutory law, has to exercise reasonable skill and care according to the specified professional standards. Providing this can be demonstrated there should be no liability for liquidated damages, for example if what is designed does fulfil its purpose due to the design. If the employer insists on and the provider signs a contract warranting 'fitness for purpose', then the provider will be liable.
- Collateral warranties: historically, the doctrine of 'privity of contract' generally means that a contract cannot confer rights or impose obligations on any person who is not party to that contract (except by tort of contract, whereby a duty of care has to be shown to exist and negligence then proved). Collateral warranties create a relationship between parties who are not in contract with

each other and normally last for 12 years from date of completion of the contract. An example may be where an employer has a new asset built, with various parts designed, supplied and installed by specialist subcontractors to the main provider, e.g. heating, cooling and ventilation. Should the parts not work, then with a collateral warranty, the employer can revert directly to the subcontractor, who if they do not remedy the situation, will be liable for liquidated damages, as opposed to the main provider.

The downside to warranties is that for a large project with many subcontractors, a myriad of additional contract terms are created, all of which add complexity and potentially cost (should lawyers be required to draft them). For this last reason, in the UK, the 'Contracts (Rights of Third Parties) Act 1999' was enacted. This allows a third party who is not under contract, but derives a benefit from that contract, to be able to enforce a term of the contract or gain financial compensation. For example, for a property developer, who has the intention to sell on a completed building to a new owner, the Act allows the new owner to enforce the contractual obligations of the provider to the property developer in, for instance, correcting defective work.

However, it was pointed out that there was an unintended consequence of the draft Act. For example, if a provider enters a contract with a government organisation as the employer, but where the beneficiaries are the general public, the effect of the Act could be that members of the public, who are only very remotely affected, can demand their rights. This could be very costly and therefore the provider would want a large premium to cover this risk. As a result, the final Act allows the parties a contract to opt out of compliance with the Act, either by expressly stating which terms are not subject to the Act or by stating a blanket opt out. If it is the latter, specific terms can be put back in by expressly stating which terms are subject to the Act and who can enforce them. Given this opt-out, a well drafted schedule of rights for third parties becomes much simpler and cheaper to put in place as an alternative to a myriad of interconnecting collateral warranties.

4.4.6 Activity 6: Issue/dispute resolution processes

There will almost always be issues that arise on contracts, most of which can be resolved by the active participants in a timely manner. However, some may not be able to be resolved and you do not want them to linger over the project, undermining relationships and distracting people from the management of current and future work.

Package contracting strategy

Consequently, employers may wish to specify a series of issue or dispute resolution procedures to be used before resorting to arbitration or litigation. It is perhaps better to label any early interventions as 'issue' resolution, because our collective experience is that people are hesitant to refer something if it is a 'dispute'. This is known as an issue or dispute ladder and starts with amicable settlements and extends up to the courts. While it is unlikely that all the stages below would be used, we have arranged them in ascending expense and hence seriousness.

- The issue is progressively escalated up the management chain of each party until agreement is hopefully reached. This happens within fixed timescales, i.e. at each level of management, the issue has to be resolved within a set timescale, otherwise it is referred upwards to the next level. Ultimately, it may get to chief executive level.
- Where the parties are still getting on, but have an issue that they just cannot agree on, non-binding expert opinion is an option. This is where an independent third party, with expertise relevant to the issue, gives a view with justification based on a short review of documents and a few discussions with the relevant people. The parties can either accept the view or use it as a basis for agreement.
- Conciliation or an executive tribunal, where an independent chair and an executive from each of the parties, who has not been directly involved in the contract, put aside a day or so to hear the facts of each party's case. They then make a decision which is acceptable to both sides bearing in mind the circumstances. If that decision proves unacceptable to one of the parties, they then proceed to the next ladder of the dispute process.
- Mediation is a process where an independent person, normally with a mediation qualification, mediates between the two parties. Often initially, they talk to one party and then the other and scuttle between the two. They isolate and take out of the equation the matters on which the parties actually agree; enable each party to see the other's perspective; and generally build consensus and agreement until the parties are sufficiently close to reach a face-to-face agreement. At this meeting, the mediator chairs.

The advantage of this approach is that the parties have ownership of the solution provided a solution is found i.e. an external expert is not 'telling' them how to sort out their differences or who was right and who was wrong. However, as the mediator cannot impose a solution, both parties need to enter into the arrangement willingly and without intransigence. It can also be quite

time consuming and therefore expensive to do, both in terms of the cost of the mediator and senior management's time in meeting him or her.
- Use of dispute avoidance/resolution boards. This comes from America where they are far more prevalent on larger projects. They have also been used on the London 2012 Olympics and other major projects. Essentially, a number of experienced professionals with a range of relevant expertise are appointed and proactively keep in touch with the contract by, for instance, reading monthly reports and periodic visits. They take a proactive role in identifying emerging issues/disputes and nipping them in the bud prior to them – and ideally avoiding them – being formally referred. If they are referred, they are much more up to speed with the circumstances leading to the dispute. The danger is that they can be perceived as already biased.

The advantage of the above five less legalistic mechanisms is that issues, and especially disputes, are rarely 'black and white', so agreements can be reached which reflect this. Further, providing the relationship between the parties is still cordial, root causes can be identified and addressed to prevent re-occurrence.

The more legal processes, which are definitely in the 'dispute' resolution arena, are:

- Adjudication:[41] This is where an experienced and usually qualified (to be an adjudicator) person is brought in to resolve an issue within a set timescale. From the initiation of the proceedings, it is usually 4 to 6 weeks before the adjudicator reports his or her decision. They consider documents submitted to them by both parties, which are always copied to the other party, and have the power to ask further questions and see further documents. Because the decision is made within a comparatively short timescale compared with arbitration or litigation, it is considered by some as 'rough and ready' justice. If your contract is considered a construction contract under the UK Housing Grants, Construction and Regeneration Act (1996) then you have to have adjudication provisions in your contract which comply with the Act (as updated by a subsequent Act), otherwise the government written Scheme for Construction Contracts applies. People in construction should note that under these Acts:

---

[41] The APM part sponsored and the Contracts and Procurement SIG contributed to *A User's Guide to Adjudication* to be published by the Construction Industry Council (CIC) in 2017. See: http://cic.org.uk/news/article.php?s=2017-02-20-cic-publishes-new-users-guide-to-adjudication

Package contracting strategy

- you have to be able to go to adjudication at any time, i.e. you could jump straight to it avoiding any of the issue resolution procedures above;
- you have to do adjudication before going to arbitration or litigation; and
- any decision of the adjudicator is enforceable unless and until over-turned by a subsequent arbitration or litigation.
■ Litigation: Where the parties – ignoring adjudication above – start the legal process which may ultimately end up in court with full legal representation. This can cost a lot of money and be very disruptive to the organisations involved. Further, the parties should note that if the court decides that one party has not tried to resolve the dispute in a constructive way, then they can award the other party's costs against that party even if they win the actual case.
■ Arbitration: Started as a cheaper, simpler, faster and less procedural form of dispute resolution compared with litigation. Here an independent and qualified arbitrator, who is knowledgeable in the type of dispute, acts like a judge. Unlike where a dispute ends up in the public courts under litigation, the arbitration is held in private (which is a big advantage) and the decision is enforceable, with appeal to the courts only being allowed in exceptional circumstances, e.g. on a point of law which is of public interest. Unfortunately, while it need not be the case, arbitration has grown to be almost as time consuming and expensive as litigation.

It is normal in a contract of any size to specify whether the final dispute resolution process is arbitration or litigation and, if the former, under what institutions procedure it will be held and where.

4.4.7 Activity 7: Choose 'best fit' standard conditions of contract if applicable

In the engineering and construction sectors there are standard forms of contract already published, often by an industry body,[42] which can cover many of the main contracting strategies and other aspects discussed in this chapter. The advantages of using a standard form of contract include:

---

[42] For instance, in the chemical industry, there is the IChemE family of forms; in the heavy engineering industry, the MF series; in building the JCT family and in civil engineering, the ICS contracts; with the NEC3 family being sufficiently flexible to apply to all the previously mentioned sectors, as well as starting to be used in the IT sector.

- They have already been written. Consequently, an employer does not need to spend time and money having them drafted from scratch.
- They have, in theory, evolved and been fine-tuned over time to take out ambiguities and inconsistencies which cause dispute. Where this is not the case, case law may exist to confirm their legal interpretation.
- There is familiarity amongst practitioners with both their interpretation and the procedures needed to operate them. In some cases, this may mean a 'better the devil you know' state of mind overrides the need for a good contract.
- The 'contra preferentum' or 'constructor against the grantor' rule will not apply to the standard terms. This rule means that when there is an ambiguity or inconsistency in the contract, e.g. where there are two ways in which a term could reasonably be interpreted, then the interpretation most favourable to the party who did not draft it is taken. In standard conditions, neither party wrote them so this does not apply. This is a significant advantage to the employer compared with drafting their own.

Consequently, where practicable, it is advisable to use a standard form of contract. However, when this is so, it is likely that some fine-tuning will be required and this is where the drafting team described in the next chapter of this guide needs to be briefed and managed properly.

4.5 Outputs

The output from this stage should be, for each package or grouping of packages by type, a briefing document for the contract drafting team and those who will detail the requirements which should inform:

- The 'best fit' contracting strategy together with any nuances or alterations not detailed below, e.g. what and how exactly the provider is to be paid, the performance testing regime, etc.
- Which standard form of contract to use (if applicable).
- The remedies to be used for each default and an indication of quantum against each.
- What risks are allocated to the employer and which are retained by the provider and if already derived, the precise wording to be used.
- The extent of any pain/gain share (if applicable).

Package contracting strategy

- The type and level of incentives, whether expressed as bonuses or damages, to be used and what measures they are payable against.
- An updated outline budget for the provider selection process.

Against all of these, a note should be supplied of why the decisions were arrived at.

The briefing document should also be written in sufficiently plain English for all those who will draft the contract to understand. This includes the technically-orientated people who will write the requirement. They will also need to know:

- Any *key terminology* to be used. For instance, in more traditional construction contracts the employer's key overseer was the 'engineer' or 'architect'. However, when the New Engineering Contract series (NEC)[43] came out, these terms were replaced with the 'project manager' and 'supervisor'. Yet many early NEC contracts documents still referred to the 'engineer' or 'architect', who do not exist in the NEC.
- The *scope of the requirement* and how it is to be expressed, e.g. is it in the form of a performance/functional specification or a fully detailed design to be implemented? The scope document should include how the delivered entity will fit in with any existing infrastructure. The scope document should detail what the provider can expect to find in terms of existing facilities, e.g. how a processing plant may link in with existing processing capabilities; what outputs from other (e.g. IT) processes are to be interfaced to, etc.
- The *constraints or boundaries* on how the provider can fulfil the requirement, e.g. in construction; hours of working, maximum noise levels, permissible access points, etc.

---

[43] New Engineering Contract (NEC) series, see www.neccontract.com.

5

Prepare the contract terms and requirements

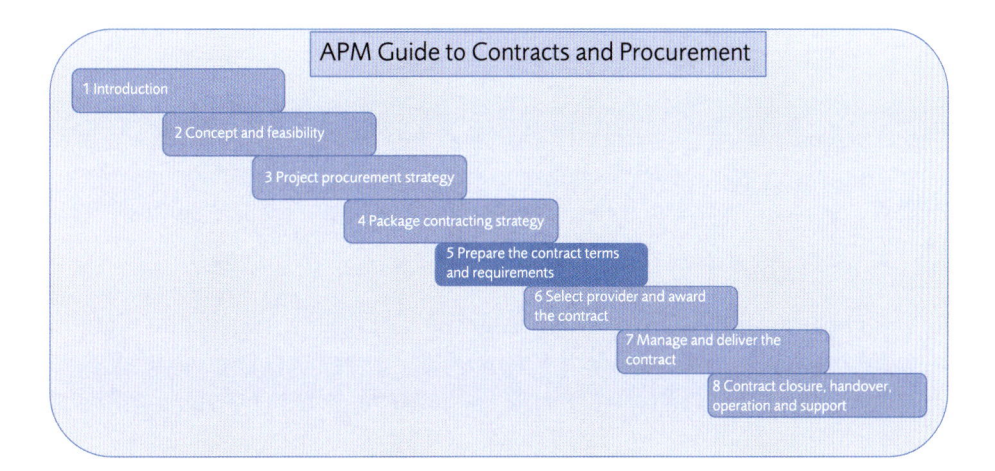

5.0 Overview

This chapter brings together the outputs from the previous stages to create a contract document that will become legally binding. The contract will include those elements described in the definition of a 'contract' given in section 1.3 previously.

During this stage the form, language and detail of the contract terms, the pricing document and the requirements are developed and finalised. These documents must be consistent; as opposed to them being entirely separate documents embodying disparate language. For instance, if the previous package contracting strategy stage (see Chapter 4) has determined that both the design and the construction of an asset should be embodied into one contract, then both the conditions of contract and requirements should reflect this.

The stage describes:

The examining of the full range of input information that may affect the contract.

APM Guide to Contracts and Procurement

- Briefing of the contract drafters.
- Determining the legal context and specific law that will govern the contract and disputes.
- Defining the contract terms (whether a standard form of contract or a custom form is to be used).
- Development of the requirements document.
- Ensuring that adequate review has taken place.

5.1 Background

Research from Canada[44] and UMIST, UK[45] in the construction and heavy engineering industries indicated that change introduced after a contract is entered into typically costs an employer three times as much as in the original contract. This highlights two factors:

1. The importance of the preceding stages in getting the 'big picture' right in terms of the business case and the deliverable required of the provider. Failure to understand this can result in large scope changes or may lead to a project which does not deliver what was required.
2. A poorly written contract and requirements document can undermine the previous stages, however well they have been done. Potentially this could cause an ongoing stream of minor changes and hence claims, which cumulatively could result in serious disruption (the 'death by a thousand cuts' syndrome) and consequential delays and additional costs. This makes it all the more important to correctly express the detail within the contract and to take care to include the appropriate level of detail to avoid ambiguity. Beware of attempting to use standard forms which do not fit the situation.

The language and detailing of both the pricing document and the requirements should follow on from the words in the conditions of contract, as opposed to them being entirely separate documents embodying disparate language. For instance, if the contract strategy has determined that both the design and the

---

[44] Revay, S. G. (1993) 'Can Construction Claims be Avoided?'.
[45] Fenn, P. and Gameson, R. (1992) Construction Conflict Management and Resolution.

Prepare the contract terms and requirements

construction of an asset should be embodied into one contract, then both the conditions of contract and requirements should reflect this.

Before developing the detail, it is worthwhile considering:

- The importance of *properly briefing* those who will do the drafting of the contract terms and requirements (as well as those who may manage and administer them) on the contents. This briefing should cover both the drafting process and the required level of technical detail in line with the procurement management plan. It is also worthwhile reviewing any available lessons learnt from previous contracts. There is often a divide between the procurement, technical and legal departments within an organisation and any recurring issues should be reviewed and care taken to avoid the same issues and errors recurring.
- *Periodic reviews* as the drafting is progressing are beneficial, as it is far better to correct a recurring mistake or systemic misunderstanding at an early stage (e.g. when only 10 per cent of a document has been completed), as opposed to correcting errors propagated through a nominally complete document at a late stage with a deadline approaching.
- There is a difference between *transaction-based* contracts and *relationship-based* contracts (see Figures 3.8). For the former, effectively one party is usually delivering already manufactured goods or low-risk defined goods or services and the other party is paying for them. In this situation, it is a relatively simple contract and therefore, apart from delivery date, price, when to pay and a description of the deliverable, there is little else to describe. For the latter, there is often a developmental component and/or significant risk which implies a need for the contracting parties to work together to manage it. Consequently, it makes sense that 'how' it is to be delivered is also covered to an appropriate level of detail and clarity, whilst not being over-prescriptive.
- For relationship based contracts, we believe the emphasis should be on the parties *solving problems* as they occur including the commercial consequences. A contract can be drafted with the emphasis being that the contract is relied-upon only when things go wrong or it can be used as a proactive working document to guide the parties' actions. If the contract is for a significant package, then things almost certainly will go wrong in some way and to some degree. Consequently, during contract execution the parties may focus their attention on recording the other party's failure to meet their contractual obligations and the resulting effects. Once the requirement has been delivered, they may then spend considerable energy constructing a claim against the

other party or defending themselves (often by counter-claiming) using the records as data to support their arguments. This is a defensive and inefficient way of behaving, although it is true that proper records should be kept.[46]

A preferable emphasis is to describe how the parties are going to work together to deliver the requirement successfully, resolving the inevitable problems that arise as it progresses. This may cover both the technical problems and any resulting commercial issues in terms of contractual ownership and any additional time and monies that the provider is entitled to. For example, it is often worth ensuring that there is a suitable section in the contract for explaining how disputes will be resolved, without resorting to litigation. As this is a guide sponsored by the Association for Project Management, we suggest that good project management principles should be embedded into the contract itself,[47] rather than being an add-on outside of (or even despite) the contract. Note that it is acceptable for the expected project management requirements to be detailed in a statement of work, being an annex forming part of the contract (with due regard to the avoidance of any contention).

- Lastly, it is worthwhile pointing out that lawyers are consultants who are experts in law. They are not necessarily experts in understanding the employer's business, the project or the related technology. Consequently, they should be briefed on this and their advice taken with due regard to the context. Lawyers are still consultants – and usually expensive ones at that – so their performance should be managed. Any deference given to the legal profession needs to be tempered by the desire to successfully deliver the requirement using good project management principles including those of managing risk and stakeholders.

5.2 Inputs

The Inputs to this stage are nominally the outputs from the previous stages plus taking due account of the requirements of the law relating to the country where

---

[46] An appropriate level of record keeping should be done efficiently as part of normal 'contract administration' not just to be relied upon if a dispute occurs when things go wrong, but also for auditing and accountability purposes generally.

[47] The most high profile exponent of this is the NEC3 family of contracts which has 'Stimulus to Good Management' as one of its explicit three high level objectives.

Prepare the contract terms and requirements

the contract is to be made. These inputs are used as the starting point for preparing the contract terms and conditions and the requirement for each contract package, or grouping of packages by type. The outputs of the previous stages described above will have been captured in the documents created; to include:

- **A signed-off business case:** An output from the concept and feasibility stage (the 'full' business case – see Chapter 2).
- **A procurement management plan**: The output from the project procurement strategy stage (see Chapter 3) including the package scope, the package interdependencies and the nature of relationship(s) to be sought with providers.
- **A briefing document:** An output from the package contracting strategy stage (see Chapter 4) used as a brief to the contract drafting team including the best-fit *contracting strategy*, the advised standard form of contract (if applicable), the remedies in case of default by a party, the risk allocation of any pain/gain share arrangement, the type and level of incentives if to be offered and the issue/dispute resolution process to be specified. In addition, any key terminology should be explained together with the scope of requirement and any constraints and boundaries.
- The **governing law** for the contract (see below).
- If used, a copy of the standard conditions of contract.

A <u>specific country</u> should be defined for the purpose of determining the governing law; in order that the further inputs described in section 5.2.1 below can be determined.

5.2.1 Law relevant to the country

> **Important disclaimer and caution: Legislation and case law is a continuously developing and highly complex subject and we stress that we can by no means cover the subject in any depth in this guide. The paragraphs below are meant to provide an outline only and we strongly advise that the legal aspects of any contract are determined in consultation with a suitably qualified and experienced lawyer.**

Governing law and jurisdiction: If choosing different countries for jurisdiction and governing law, the courts in a given jurisdiction may choose to ignore the other countries governing or possibly give eccentric interpretations of it. This should be taken into account in selecting jurisdictions.

If negotiating a contract with an unfamiliar governing law, you will almost certainly need local legal support; even if only to carry out periodic risk assessments and health-checks of the contract.

Even within the UK, you should specify whether it is the law of England and Wales, Scotland, or Northern Ireland that applies. Regardless of which country's law is chosen, it should always be stated in the contract. Legal advice should be taken to decide on the appropriate country of jurisdiction.

5.2.1.1 UK case law and legislation

All of the following impose specific legal requirements on the procurement of a project; whereas the rest of the guide is 'guidance', the following are all legal 'requirements'. In many cases the duties to comply cannot be contracted out by the employer to the provider and the employer, in many cases, remains the duty holder with specific actions upon them.

Contract law is based on court judgments over the centuries. In more recent years statutes and other legislation have also impacted on contract law. The effect of this impact is usually felt in one of two ways:

- Legislation implying terms into the contract, or limiting or affecting what is allowed in the contract.
- Legislation which is relevant to the deal and which needs to be catered for in the contract.

UK legislation affecting contract terms includes:

- Unfair Contract Terms Act 1977: This sets out various statutory provisions; of which the most relevant are those imposing limitations on the extent to which one can limit one's liability in different types of contract.
- Sale of Goods Act 1979, Supply of Goods and Services Act 1982, Sale and Supply of Goods Act 1994, Unfair Terms in Consumer Contract Regulations 1999 and Unfair Terms in Consumer Contracts (Amendment) Regulations 2000: All set out various implied warranties (some of which cannot be excluded) as to title (in plain English this means ownership and when it

Prepare the contract terms and requirements

is transferred) of standard of goods sold or supplied and services provided. Drafters need to be aware of the extent to which, legally, certain statutory provisions can give way to the express terms of the contract (e.g. warranty periods). If buyers are not familiar with this, experienced sellers certainly are.
- Competition Act 1998: This, among other things, embodies relevant provisions of the EU Treaty seeking to prevent anti-competitive arrangements and agreements. An important aspect of the Enterprise Act 2002 is that professional services (e.g. those provided by architects, lawyers and accountants) are now subject to the same competition requirements as manufacturing and other service companies.
- Contracts (Rights of Third Parties) Act 1999: Since the introduction of this Act, it is now possible to confer positive rights (not obligations) on parties who are not signatories to the contract, principally the right to enforce any terms on performance of duties. Any rights to third parties can be excluded but this must be expressly written into the contract.
- Equal Pay Act (1970) and Equality Act (2010): The 1970 act covers equal pay between men and women and is largely superseded by the Equality Act (2010). The latter act is based on the EU Equal Treatment Directives and expands the UK legislation to cover race relations, disability discrimination in addition to sexual discrimination.

UK legislation, which may require the parties to include specific obligations and provisions in the contract, could include:

- Data Protection Act 1998 (and a raft of regulations): This sets strict rules on the processing and handling of data, in particular on sensitive personal data and leads to sensitivities where personal data is to be exported outside the European Economic Area. The Act also requires certain provisions to be included in contracts where data processors are being used.
- Freedom of Information Act 2000 (public sector contracts only): Imposes extensive obligations on public bodies to provide information in response to requests. The timescales for responding are challenging (20 days). Typical issues in project agreements are:
    - The extent to which pricing and related information should be exempt from disclosure, and
    - Compliance with the required timescale for employer responses to information requests.

- Transfer of Undertaking (Protection of Employment) Regulations 2006 and as amended in 2014 ('TUPE'): Setting out provisions dealing with the potential transfer of staff on the transfer of an undertaking and protecting their rights in various ways. TUPE can be an issue both on commencement and termination of a project (usually outsourcing or managed services contracts) and can have a significant financial impact.
- Health and safety regulations: This is a huge area and it is worthwhile noting that personal liability for negligence now extends to individual directors and organisations. A number of industries have specific legislation which applies to their sector. Note that effective from February 2016 the sentencing regime has also changed, with unlimited fines and jail sentences available for most forms of breach.
- Building regulations and town and country planning issues: The Town and Country Planning Act (1990) and local council regulations.
- Environmental legislation: There is an extensive list of regulations that may apply. A sample list of such legislation is given below:
    - Water Resources Act (1991)(Amendment) Regulations (2009)
    - Water Industry Act (1991)
    - Environmental Civil Sanctions Order (2010) SI1157 and Environmental Civil Sanctions (Miscellaneous Amendments) Regulations (2010)
    - Capital Allowances (Environmentally Beneficial Plant and Machinery) Order (2003), as amended
    - Environmental Damage (Prevention and Remediation) (Amendment) Regulations (2010) SI 587
    - Environmental Protection Act (1990)
    - The Hazardous Waste (England and Wales) Regulations 2005, as amended
    - Climate Change Act (2008)
    - The Clean Neighbourhoods and Environment Act (2005)
    - Environment provision of the Town and Country Planning Act (1990)
    - Environment Protection (Duty of Care) Regulations (2014)
- Legislation relating to electronic contracts, e.g. The Electronic Commerce (EC Directive) Regulations (2002).
- The Bribery Act (2010): Covering all acts of bribery undertaken by employees and agents of a company. Fines can be very significant (e.g. 10 per cent of its worldwide parent company gross revenues) for unethical conduct.
- The Modern Slavery Act (2015): Covering slavery, servitude, compulsory labour and human trafficking.

Prepare the contract terms and requirements

Bear in mind also that case law, as well as setting rules of interpretation of clauses (see Activity 7 of this stage), sometimes goes further and sets rules on what can and cannot be contracted for and for what can be bindingly enforced by a contract. Examples relevant for major projects include rules limiting the enforceable length of non-solicitation clauses and rules making contracts for illegal purposes unenforceable.

5.2.1.2 International law and law of a foreign country (if relevant)

Procurement with an international dimension not only adds complexity to the management of a project, but also needs careful consideration on the legal front. The issues can be broken down into:

- Which country's governing law should apply?
- Which country's or countries' courts should have jurisdiction in the event of litigation?
- What impact will a given country's custom and practice have on the content of the contract, how it is negotiated and how it is performed?

Jurisdiction: Where the parties to a contract come from different countries or are to perform the contract in a different country from their own, real problems can arise in establishing which courts should have jurisdiction. There are various conventions and treaties which set out rules to apply in establishing this against the relevant factors, often including the domicile of the parties, where the contract is to be performed and what the parties have agreed.

It is very important to get this right: There is a real risk that, regardless of what the parties have agreed in the contract about jurisdiction and governing law, a given country's courts may decide that they have jurisdiction and will hear the case with their own views on how the contract should be interpreted. In some cases, you cannot remove this risk entirely because the relevant countries may not be signatories to treaties or conventions on these issues.

As well as agreeing and stating the jurisdiction, you need to think about how to enforce judgment; agreeing to be able to sue in the UK may be of little use if all the pertinent assets are in another country. There are extensive international agreements on mutual enforcement of judgments (so courts in country 'A' will often agree to enforce judgments from courts in country 'B' and vice versa). A further degree of complexity comes from the fact that countries also have international agreements on enforcement, arbitration and other non-litigation dispute resolution measures and these do not always mirror agreements on enforcement of court judgments. Consider mentioning the use of Incoterms, for where certain materials may be being imported from overseas.[48]

Custom and practice: The practices built up in different countries over the years, including the influence of governing law, will affect how the contract is performed, which in turn may affect what you need to agree in the contract. Similarly, different countries often develop different approaches to various contractual, commercial and risk areas, and bridging this gap can cause difficulties. Again, local advice can be invaluable in guiding you through this.

Different governing law will also set different rules for what terms are enforceable and how they are interpreted. For instance, in most of the world stated liquidated damages for poor performance cannot exceed a genuine pre-estimate of likely loss. However, in the USA and Middle East, they can be punitive; also, take advice on the effect of cross-border taxation and the treatment of sales/goods/value-added taxes where companies trade internationally. Ensure that gross costs are understood, if you are used to normally dealing with costs ex-VAT.

Lastly, to point out the obvious, just because the law of contract is, say, that of England and Wales (or of Scotland or Northern Ireland), does not mean other laws of the country in which it is wholly or partly being performed do not apply (e.g. local health and safety obligations, employee relations law, etc.). Many UK Acts have cross territorial application, for example bribery and corruption laws.

5.3 Activities

The process is illustrated in Figure 5.1.

5.3.1 Activity 1: Brief the drafters of the contract terms and requirement

At a minimum, those drafting the contract terms and detailing the requirement must have access and full understanding of the chosen package contracting strategy, which includes a full understanding of the current standing of the

---

[48] http://www.iccwbo.org/products-and-services/trade-facilitation/incoterms-2010/.

Prepare the contract terms and requirements

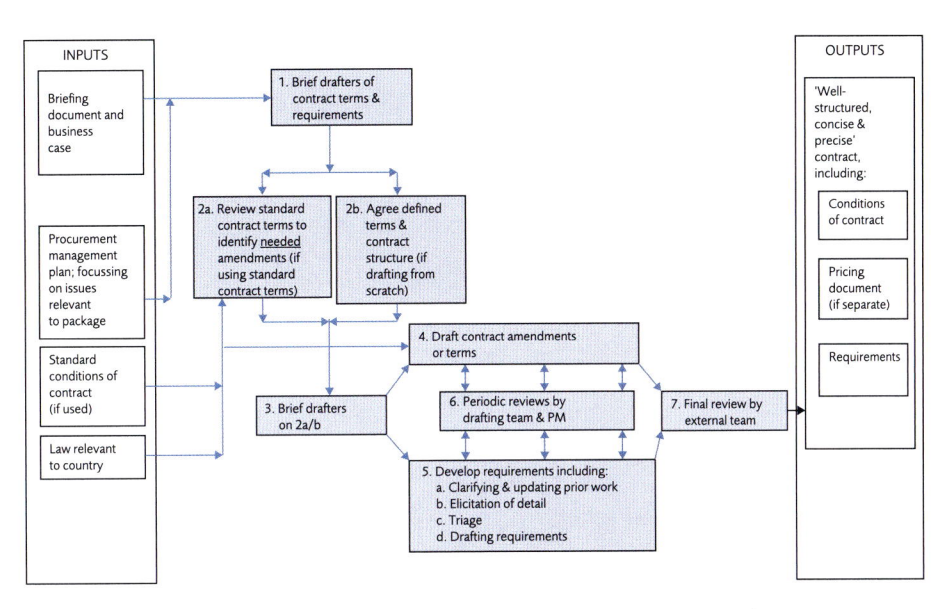

Figure 5.1 Process diagram for the prepare contract terms and requirements stage

package scope and its interactions and interdependencies with others. Otherwise, we have seen, for instance, they may well enthusiastically develop a fully defined requirement, in terms of goods and services specified when actually the contract requires a performance specification. Failure to have this initial understanding can result in significant wasted professional time being expended, which not only costs in fees, but delays the overall project. Make sure that the responsibility for design and specification rests where it best suits the employer's requirements. Contract forms or procurement routes can sometimes be inadvertently selected.

In addition, unless there are sound commercial reasons not to, it is suggested that drafters are also briefed on the business case and the procurement management plan as well as having access to the relevant documents. This is to ensure that they understand the 'big picture' of the project, how their part fits into it and have a full understanding of the inter-dependencies of their contract package across the project. The drafters should also be given a list of the names and contact details for those parties with whom they are expected to liaise to obtain answers to questions arising for the detail. This may be an extensive list where the contract is complex or international.

5.3.2 Activity 2: Draft the conditions of contract

Activity 2 is split into the two possibilities:

- Selection of a standard form of contract; if it is decided to use a standard form.
- Drafting specific terms; if a standard form of contract is not used.

5.3.2.1 Activity 2a: Choose standard conditions of contract

If using standard conditions of contract, review the standard conditions for alignment with the procurement management plan, identifying amendments which *need* to be made.

As stated in the previous chapter in Activity 7, there are a number of good reasons for using standard conditions of contract. The more they are adjusted, the more these advantages decline (and any advantage gained may even disappear). Adjustments to standard terms may render the resulting contract (terms, requirement, payment document, etc.) unwieldy and unclear; possibly containing ambiguity and inconsistencies, which do not aid the successful delivery of a contract or project which it covers.

If it is anticipated that standard terms need to be adjusted, we suggest that, as a project manager or project procurement professional, a tight rein is kept on any changes. In the real world, there are always unexpected risks that cannot be totally excluded and removed by legal drafting, although legal professionals will attempt to do this. The reality is that legal drafting does not remove risks, it just transfers or shares contractual ownership and hence which party takes the first order effects, but the employer often takes – or shares – the second and third order effects. For example, while the provider might have damages if they deliver their contract late, the employer's contract/project is still late, which may well have impact on operations, reputation etc.

So beware spending lots of time doing this. Good planning and drafting can reduce the risks but the cost of preparing a theoretically all-embracing contract has to be weighed against the cost and delay due to its creation, not to mention the prolonged duration trying to get the other party to accept all of the terms. For instance, a 500-page contract document, describing rights, obligations and remedies for non-performance would be an overkill for a 10-page requirement specifying goods. We suggest that a team leader responsible for the development of the requirement is involved in the review process to guard against overkill when developing the contract.

Prepare the contract terms and requirements

In the course of drafting, we suggest that:

- Rigorous monitoring is undertaken to ensure that additional amendments are not surreptitiously introduced.
- Rigorous change control needs to be adopted for any amendments.

5.3.2.2 Activity 2b: Specifically drafted conditions of contract

If drafting contract terms from scratch, then *agree the defined terms and the structure of the contract* prior to drafting the detail.

NB: Developing bespoke terms can be very expensive so make sure that if this option is chosen there is a real tangible benefit to doing so. Unless a strong relationship is developed with the provider it is also likely that agreeing the terms will take longer because they will be unfamiliar with them.

In this instance, we mean of the whole contract, including the requirements and not just the contract terms. The risk of omitting key provisions which would automatically have been included in standard contracts must be considered, along with the extra time and cost of actually doing the drafting work for new clauses. It is very important that working protocols on terminology and structure are established early on and communicated as there will be no prior models or templates to fall back on. 'Defined terms' are the key terms of the contract which will be repeated throughout the contract, both in the conditions of contract and requirements. Before any work is done, it is therefore worthwhile agreeing these and the overall contract structure.

The above is simple to say, but requires considerable thought and time to get right.

5.3.3 Activity 3: Brief the drafting team and those detailing the requirements on 2a/b

If standard conditions of contract are being used, there is a need to ensure that those who will be detailing the requirements are able to understand its terminology and structure before they commence drafting. They may already have knowledge and previous experience and if so may need little briefing. Previously used successful approaches often offer the lowest risk, e.g. how the technical requirement is structured.

The drafting team will need to have an understanding of any relevant amendments and of the agreed structure for the requirements. If, during the briefing, valid suggestions for improvement are made, they should be considered. Do not immediately agree to make changes: it is better to think through the impacts first. It would be preferable, though, to agree these changes early on rather than introducing changes and revisions to make the contract work when much has already been written.

If the contract terms are being drafted from scratch, the drafting team will need to be briefed on the defined terms and the contract structure.

5.3.4 Activity 4: Draft contract terms or amendments

Both the contract terms and the requirements should be:

- *Well structured*; so that participants know where to find relevant information.
- *Concise*; so that having found the relevant section or paragraph, it is not necessary to wade through unnecessary flannel or legalese.
- *Precise*; so that what is required is adequately described (without over-specifying, which restricts innovation). We often find that obligations may be expressed in abstract legal terms that could be ambiguous. It is essential to express, in tangible terms, WHO has to do WHAT, WHERE and by WHEN.

An understanding of the above should mean that each party better understands what is expected of them, which in turn should lessen the chances of any failure to perform thereby resulting in potentially reducing the number of disputes. If problems do arise, the clarity of contract terms and requirements usually leads to a speedier resolution. Any ambiguities can lead to protracted disputes where one party may interpret a clause to its advantage whilst the other party may interpret it in another way as being to their advantage.

> **OUR TOP 7 DRAFTING TIPS FOR THE CONTRACT TERMS AND REQUIREMENTS**
>
> 1. Make obligations clear – use 'shall/will' and not 'it is our intention', 'we propose' or 'it is expected'.
> 2. Keep it as simple as you can – most project undertakings are complicated enough without adding unnecessary complexity.
> 3. Keep language and terms consistent – contracts are not literary works and do not require a variety of expression. Ideally, state things only once

and refer back to the original statement. This avoids any small changes that are introduced causing ambiguity and inconsistency.
4. Take account of the 'rules of interpretation' (see Activity 7).
5. Work through processes and consequences – what happens if something is not done or not agreed?
6. Keep the drafting team size to a manageable number. If sharing the work, plan up front in detail who is doing what and what the drafting conventions are.
7. Get the members of the drafting team to review each other's work – this helps ensure clarity and consistency of style, language, terms, etc. as the drafting of the contract progresses. Even if something is written by one expert for another expert, its meaning should still be clear to an informed non-expert *and* be contractually correct.

5.3.5 Activity 5: Develop the requirements

To varying degrees, the requirements will have been partially developed in the previous stages. We re-iterate that now is the time to specify it to a level of detail which:

- Ensures that the employer will receive a package of works, goods or services that are fit for the employer's purpose. This aspect needs to be viewed from both the employer's viewpoint and the potential provider's viewpoint i.e. how they will read it.
- Allows the provider as much leeway in what is provided and how it is provided in order to achieve greatest value for money for the employer.
- Matches the strengths of the party who will be delivering it, e.g. for a new construction asset, there is little point in specifying all the benefits that the employer hopes to receive from it if the constructor only has construction expertise and is building what has been designed by a third party.

Developing the requirement has four stages:

1. **Clarification and updating of the package scope and interdependencies:** This includes confirming the employer's and other stakeholders' strategic goals as relating to the project and package objectives, and

verifying and clarifying of any potentially conflicting or ambiguous statements regarding the package.

2. **Elicitation of detail:** To the level determined in the procurement management plan for how the requirement will be expressed. Key steps within this stage are to:

   a. Agree techniques for soliciting requirements, e.g. value engineering techniques, problem analysis, 'board blasting'/brainstorming, Ishikawa (cause and effect) diagrams, structured interviews, etc., from which a programme of work can be established.

   b. Implement effective fact-finding processes through interviews or workshops.

   c. Identify features which are:
      i. **Needed:** What has to be in the requirement for it to be fit for purpose?
      ii. **Wanted:** What would add value to the project and make it better if accommodated?
      iii. **Nice to have:** What is on the 'wish list'?

3. **Triage:** Decide which features are appropriate to include in the requirement. It is rarely possible to include every requested feature gathered during the elicitation activity due to disparate priorities, limited resources, time-to-market demands and risk intolerance. Deciding what should be in the requirement should be judged by the project sponsor and the ultimate users, facilitated by the project manager. Inclusion criteria should be used to arrive at an agreed set of desired and realistic requirements. This may be achieved by:

   a. Identifying criteria for inclusion, e.g. technical feasibility.
   b. Testing for a requirement, e.g. asking if it is a description of an output.
   c. Normalising requirements, e.g. discarding duplication, omissions or ambiguity.
   d. Testing all of the above with the employer and other stakeholders.

   Take care to ensure that the phraseology used to define the requirement matches the type of specification you are seeking to use, e.g. beware of brand preference. For instance, if you are using a performance specification, but specify a component that has to be used and the asset then does not meet the performance requirement, the provider may well argue that the component specified is the reason and hence not liable for the lack of performance.

4. **Detailing of the requirements:** Much that was said in section 5.3.4 about drafting the contract terms (Activity 4) also applies to drafting the requirement in terms of practical tips that were given for drafting. The key

point is that if the previous steps have been followed, then the detailing of the requirement becomes much easier and a much better requirement normally results.

5.3.6 Activity 6: Periodic reviews by the drafting team and the project manager

This should include review of the drafting teams' work by an appointed and qualified peer delegate. The objective is for errors or misunderstandings to be picked up early and resolved, rather than being allowed to propagate throughout the whole contract documents or the parts that an individual is writing. Review levels may be from informal 'buddy reviews' through to systematic reviews which are identified in the project plan for the drafting work. A good test would be to discover if a person with some knowledge and experience of what is being drafted, but by no means an expert or specialist, understands what is required and how it is to be delivered.

5.3.7 Activity 7: External review

At a minimum, there needs to be an external review performed once the contract terms and/or requirements are thought to be complete. It is strongly suggested that there should also be periodic external reviews to catch errors early in the process. External reviewers should ideally be personnel that have had some involvement in the earlier stages of drafting, as this ensures an understanding of what the contract is about. External reviewers also need to have sufficient legal and/or technical knowledge to be able to competently understand the relevant documents.

Apart from comparing the requirement, however expressed, with what is the desired outcome for the contract, reviewers of both the contract terms and of the requirement (and for that matter the drafters) should ask themselves the following questions:

- *Are there clauses that over-constrain the providers' ability to deliver; and hence potentially increase costs and timescales?* Two simple questions can be asked to challenge constraints:
  a. **'Who or what states that we must or must not do this?'**: This question should identify the source of the constraint. The source may be a

legal requirement or 'rule' of the employer organisation. Alternatively the source may be questionable; being perhaps, a local practice. subjective interpretation or based on an invalid assumption.

   b. **'What would happen if this constraint was relaxed?'**: This question identifies the consequences of relaxing the constraint and may usefully expand the leeway that the providers are allowed to deliver the contract. As a result, potential providers may be less constrained in utilising their inherent expertise, resulting in improved delivery timescales and/or reduced prices.

- *What's missing?* It's easy to evaluate and critique what is in front of you. Stand back when looking both at the overall content and each section and ask what, if anything, have we missed that we should cover? Having said this, do not add additional rules which over-constrain the provider and add cost.
- *Are the rules of interpretation (sometimes called 'rules of construction') at the forefront of your mind?* These are highlighted in the box below. It should be noted that this list is not exhaustive, but can be a pointer to the most common causes of disputes over the meaning of drafted clauses. To some extent, the principles below overlap each other and some may conflict in practice. In this sense, they are not 'rules' but potentially conflicting principles. The legal interpretation of a poorly written contract can be problematic; causing arguments and counter-arguments to a certain interpretation. The solution is a well-written contract that is 'well-structured, concise and precise', with its intentions openly and unambiguously stated in the contract documents. In practice, this is harder to achieve than simply stating it as an objective.

> **Rules of interpretation:** Should a dispute go to court, the purpose of the rules of interpretation or construction of contracts is to discover the intention of the parties, as expressed in their acts and words. Over the years, certain rules of interpretation have developed with case law and statute. The objective of stating them here is to avoid a contractual dispute developing in the first place.
>
> (1) Intentions are gathered from the words and conduct of the parties in making the contract. Consequently:

Prepare the contract terms and requirements

- A 'secret' unexpressed intention has no relevance.
- If something is not stated or there is ambiguity in how it is stated, then intention can be implied from the conduct of the parties.
- Equally, where there is omission or ambiguity, intention can be implied from the recitals, e.g. documents given as background to the contract.

(2) Words will be construed to have an ordinary meaning, unless it can be shown they are mutually understood by the parties to have a special sense. This 'special sense' could be by custom or usage in a particular industry or sector. It could also be by reference to defined terms stated in the contract.

(3) Each party will be presumed to have used the words in the context in which the other party was entitled to understand them, i.e. a contract should be written to be understandable from the other parties' perspective, because that is how it will be interpreted in the courts (see below).

(4) The words employed will be construed most strongly against the party using them. This means that if there are two reasonable interpretations of a set of words, one of which favours the employer and one of which favours the contracting party and it is the former who has written the contract, then the interpretation which favours the contracting party prevails.

(5) All parts of the contract will be construed together and the general intent thereby asserted will govern the interpretation of particular words and phrases. For instance, if in 9 out of 10 places in the contract, it states that a party shall do something in one way and in one part it says do it another way which contradicts this, the general – the 9 out 10 – will apply. However, if the '1 out of 10' has a specific circumstance attached to it, then it would apply in the specific circumstance only (see point (8) below).

(6) Hand-written words will prevail over printed ones where in conflict. The reason behind this is that the parties show their real intention by hand-writing in words, even though they may not have erased the printed word by mistake or oversight. Include any post tender discussions and verbal agreements in a summary document to be included as an appendix to the contract.

> Consider including example scenarios in the terms of the contract to clarify what terms mean in practice.
>
> (7) Printed or hand-written words prevail over verbally stated words or records of what was said, e.g. in pre-contract negotiations. This is because it is far easier to prove what is written than to interpret two different parties' recollection of what was said.
>
> (8) Detail overrides generality: If in a part of a contract, it states that in particular circumstances that a party shall do 'X', whereas in a more general statement it states they shall do 'Y', then 'X' shall prevail in the particular circumstances. Consequently, the particular circumstances need to be described sufficiently, so that it is clear when 'X' applies. An example of this in one standard form of conditions of contract is a general statement that 'subcontractor's people and construction equipment are treated in the same way as those of the main provider'. The specific exception is for claims and variations when they are treated differently, but only for the purpose of pricing those claims and variations.

One means of reducing uncertainty in interpretation *between* contractual documents is to state the order of precedence of contractual documents. This provides that if there is ambiguity between two documents, the one with the higher precedence effectively overrides the lesser document.

Another mechanism for reducing uncertainty is the use of an 'entire agreement' clause. This guards against the potential for any pre-contract discussions or un-referenced documents to be construed as being part of the contract, when that was neither party's intention. An 'entire agreement' clause ensures that only the documents referenced form part of the agreement or contract and not any others, e.g. verbal agreements, notes of meetings recording agreements or tender clarifications. It can be as simple as stating in a conditions of contract clause something like "This contract is the entire agreement between the parties." The reader should note that this does not exclude liability for fraudulent misrepresentation, i.e. knowingly lying (which is also a criminal offence) and, without further additional clauses, negligent misrepresentation, e.g. making a statement which you think is true without having exercised due skill and care in checking the facts or arriving at an opinion.

5.4 Outputs

The outputs from this stage should be 'well-structured, concise and precise' documents as follows:

- Contract terms.
- Pricing document (if separate).
- Requirements.

These documents can be used for either tendering or single-source negotiation, which is described in Chapter 6.

6

Select provider and award the contract

APM Guide to Contracts and Procurement
- 1 Introduction
- 2 Concept and feasibility
- 3 Project procurement strategy
- 4 Package contracting strategy
- 5 Prepare the contract terms and requirements
- 6 Select provider and award the contract
- 7 Manage and deliver the contract
- 8 Contract closure, handover, operation and support

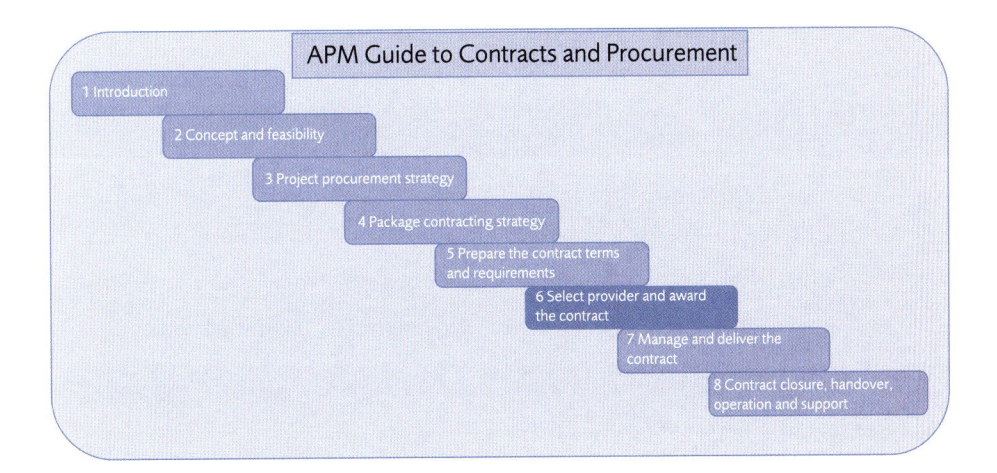

6.0 Overview

In this stage, the 'best value' available provider(s) for the individual contracted-out project packages are selected and the contract awarded to them. This stage is particularly key, as once the contract(s) are placed, the legally binding commitments will have been made and external costs will start accruing.

During this stage, a more detailed view is taken of what criteria are used to shortlist and select the potential provider(s) given what they will be asked to deliver in the contract, including risks allocated to them and other factors such as market conditions.

The stage includes:

- Definition of the selection criteria, which may include factors such as track record, price and experience of personnel.
- The process that needs to be implemented based on the overall timescales of the project or programme.

- The discipline that must be exercised in interactions with potential providers to avoid prejudicing any competition, entering into a contract inadvertently and/or under different terms than intended.

In this chapter, we describe an intensive selection process that would be due on a significant contract. For smaller procurements, the process can be tailored to be appropriately cost effective and may not have as many stages. The available budget for the selection process should have been initially estimated during the project procurement strategy stage (see Chapter 3) and refined as necessary during the package contracting strategy stage (see Chapter 4). Further adjustment may be necessary during the selection process as more information comes to light from the informed parties involved (see section 6.4.2).

There are legal regulations governing the selection of providers, including UK Acts of Parliament governing public procurement and EU directives (as summarised in section 5.2.1). Consequently, it is necessary to check that the process adopted does not contravene any such legislation and we therefore strongly recommend that specialist advice is obtained to ensure compliance.

6.1 Background

'Best value' is a term often bandied around and can mean many things to different people within organisations and projects. Under EU procurement terminology, a term used is the most economically advantageous tender (MEAT).[49] It should be understood that best value is not limited to cost but can be better thought of as obtaining the most benefit (in terms of cost, time quality and risk) given the resource used to get that benefit. Whichever term applies, it normally involves some combination of the following five factors:

- <u>What</u> are we buying (what are we getting for our money)?
- <u>How</u> are we going to obtain it? In a project environment, where delivery happens over a period of time and often interacts with other live services or assets, the 'how' of delivery can be just as important as the end result (<u>what</u> you get).
- <u>When</u> are we getting it (especially if there are programme dependencies)?

---

[49] http://www.europarl.europa.eu/news/en/news-room/20140110BKG32432/new-eu-rules-on-public-procurement-ensuring-better-value-for-money.

Select provider and award the contract

- How much will it <u>cost</u>? And this further splits down into purchase cost and whole life cost.
- An acceptable level of uncertainty associated with the above factors. This is about <u>assurance</u> and the 'comfort factor'.

The relative importance of these factors depends on the nature of the deliverables being provided:

- A time critical deliverable might be a school to be ready to service the increasing population of children for a particular catchment.
- A quality critical deliverable might be upstream valves for an oil rig (and what happens if they go wrong (viz. Deepwater Horizon Oil Spill of 2010[50])).

In the value continuum:

- At one extreme, if the employer is specifying commonly available low technology goods to be delivered by a certain date, then providing the goods meet the technical specification, they will primarily be selected on lowest purchase cost.
- At the other extreme, for a unique and innovative package which is critical to the success of the overall project, then the likely out turn cost will be only one of many factors considered.

Thought, therefore, should be given to what, precisely, *best value* means when selecting a provider for an individual contract and the best process for ensuring that is what the employer gets. The Kraljic matrix of section 3.3.6 is worth considering to help determine the most appropriate relationship when deciding on a selection approach.

6.1.1 Principles of an effective and efficient selection process

Both for the successful delivery of the contract and for subsequent contracts, it is imperative that the selection process is:

- *Clear*, with a degree of transparency, and hence unbiased (and perceived to be so). If this is not the case, the reputational risk of the employer organisation

[50] Encyclopaedia Britannica (2010) Deepwater Horizon Oil Spill of 2010.

can suffer both in the general eyes of stakeholders, e.g. press, public, politicians etc., and in the eyes of those organisations that may bid for future work. If not so, then they will either not bid or put in high prices for future work. To this end, it is wise to identify the selection criteria in advance of putting the tender documents together, and not once responses are received. It is not necessary to publish the selection criteria unless it is a public works tender (when it is an absolute must). Publishing can lead to bidders concentrating solely on 'answering' the weighting matrix and not giving an 'honest and natural' response.

- *Documented*, so that a decision can be justified both internally and, if necessary, externally.
- *Relevant*, in terms of any questions asked are pertinent to the specific contract. Having said this, the earlier filtering questions on relevant experience and financial standing are likely to be more general, while the final questions should be specific to the package.
- *Proportionate*, in terms of the value of the contract that will be awarded and the effort needed to both answer and mark them. By value, we do not just mean cost, but benefit and risks to the overall project. Do remember that external effort is expended by each and every one of the potential providers, which for all but one will be largely wasted effort, and that each submission needs to be marked by internal resource. There are a number of electronic and web-based tendering tools available which can be used for the administration of the tender process. A useful guideline document on e-tendering is provided by Cooperative Research Centres (CRC) Australia.[51] These can significantly reduce the time required to analyse bids, as well as help ensure consistency of fair and equal communications during the bid.

Having said the above, do:

- Consider the consequences of getting the wrong provider through running too lightweight a competition. Selection of the 'wrong' provider could lead to poor quality, delays and disruption to other packages and additional un-budgeted costs.
- Always undertake an element of post tender review and analysis, to clarify bids, and re-visit if necessary.

---

[51] Kajewski, S. (2006) *Guidelines for Successful eTendering Implementation*.

- Avoid the easy option of 'automatic' selection based on, for instance: unsubstantiated opinion; the existing incumbent providing satisfactory performance only when others could provide superior performance etc. What appears to be a 'no-brain' choice may end up as excessively costly. An objective review is essential. It is best to solicit independent input outside of the project team. Often other parts of the employer's business can have a very different impression of a 'favoured' provider.

In addition, the process needs to protect bidding organisations' intellectual property rights and project specific solutions that give them competitive advantage. At the very least, ground rules and protocols for what, how and when information from an individual tenderer is shared – if at all – need to be established upfront (see section 6.1.4 below).

6.1.2 Legal compliance red flags

As we pointed out in section 6.0, due regard needs to be given to the regulation of provider selection and the process should be checked against the applicable legislation by a legal representative. In addition, diligence needs to be given to the behaviour of providers as contravention of compliance regulations governing aspects such as such as health and safety, environment, bribery, modern slavery, etc. Appendix C provides a list of 'red flags' where a provider's behaviour might suggest contravention.

6.1.3 Ownership, governance and personnel

The first fundamental need is to allocate the ownership of the selection process to a named individual. This could be for the overall project, e.g. the project manager, who may then delegate the selection process for each individual package or category of packages to a named deputy.

However, given the previously identified principles for an effective and efficient selection process, for each competition it is necessary that there is some sort of check and balance, both to ensure that:

- The selection criteria used and process match the above principles.
- At the various stages of down selection, including final award, they are fairly applied without favouritism or bias.

APM Guide to Contracts and Procurement

This implies that for whoever is doing the administration and scoring of the proposals, there is always someone above them who is checking. For instance:

- If it is a small project with the selection process being run by the project manager, then the process, selection criteria and scoring and marking thereof are signed off by the project sponsor.
- If it is a procurement specialist, then they are signed off by the project manager.
- Larger packages, especially with subjective criteria such as written texts, presentations, site visits etc. are marked by consensus.
- Key packages on larger projects – or categories of packages – are signed off by a provider selection panel (PSP), which may include some members of the project board or steering group.
- A formal sign-off template/report should, ideally, be prepared for the project (an example template is provided in Appendix B).

These checks should not be line by line re-scoring, but sufficient to ensure the previously mentioned principles are adhered to in practice and that the bid will meet project/package objectives.

6.1.4 Communications control

Information of significance to the employer and the respective providers will need to be passed between them in order to carry out the selection process. Factors to be seriously considered are:

- maintaining the confidentiality of information; and
- ensuring bidders are given equitable access to information to maintain fairness.

In order to control the flow of information a person needs to be in the role of 'communications controller' whether as a dedicated role or not. The communications controller will have the responsibility of being the primary point-of-contact (PoC) and also for keeping communication records being appropriately segregated.

6.1.4.1 Confidentiality

The confidentiality of information supplied to the employer by providers and vice versa is to be respected. Individual companies' intellectual property (IP) can be a

Select provider and award the contract

valuable source of competitive advantage and needs to be respected and appropriately controlled by all involved parties. It is therefore imperative that a communications protocol is set up between the employer and each of the potential providers. Key features typically include protocols on what the parties can share with other, primarily:

- Information that is confidential to the employer, which is not to be distributed outside the potential providers and their bid teams.
- Answers to clarifications on the conditions of contract and the requirement.
- Individual tenderers' IP and proposed project specific solutions.

In this respect, non-disclosure agreements (NDA's) should be put in place at an early stage in the selection process, which protect all parties' interests. Newcomers to the selection team need to be informed of the terms of these NDAs and the whole selection team periodically reminded, so that terms are not inadvertently broken during or following any face-to-face interaction with potential providers. A secure process is needed to store and respond to questions and clarifications. This may well require infrastructure, such as a secure internal file-server.

The obligations of the Data Protection Act 1998 (see section 5.2.1.1) must also be observed should any information be of a personal nature (e.g. outline curriculum vitaes (CVs) of project teams).

6.1.4.2 Information sharing

Fairness must be observed by providing information equitably between providers to exclude the possibility of any bias. Where clarification questions are addressed, it is necessary to share such questions and answers with all bidders, having removed the private details. Sufficient time for responses should be allowed for all parties to respond.

At each stage of the down selection, it is also necessary to inform successful and unsuccessful candidates, which avoids unsuccessful providers wasting their time (this courtesy also helps to maintain relationships). Unsuccessful bidders should be given brief feedback on why they have been unsuccessful. An e-tendering tool (see section 6.1.1) can automate and significantly simplify this process and also provide traceable electronic records.

For a contract with a public authority the provisions of the Freedom of Information Act 2000 must also be observed (see section 5.2.1.1).

6.1.4.3 Selection team make-up

In a project environment where the employer's and provider's personnel may well be working alongside each other, we recommend that the core of the team that runs the selection process should include those who will work alongside the chosen provider. This will provide continuity and avoid steep learning curves during delivery. During selection, it is also necessary to involve specialist personnel including:

- Procurement professionals to review the process, e.g. to ensure appropriate protocols and regulations are observed such as EU procurement rule.
- Subject matter experts, who can be called in as and when needed or desirable.

> **Subject matter experts:** Users with subject matter knowledge and expertise who may contribute to defining requirements and acceptance criteria. *APM Body of Knowledge 6th edition*

Note that such specialist focus can be quite narrow, therefore they need to be briefed on the big picture of the project, how the individual package fits into it and the critical aspects of that package.

6.2 Risk management

The use of externally contracted resources impacts risk level associated with a project. This level of risk is geared to the level of dependency on the provider(s). The necessary risk management plan should include:

- Technical risks that are specific to the work being undertaken by the prospective provider and that can be obtained from its own risk register.
- Technical risks, owned by the employer, associated with the dependencies on the success of the provider in containing its risks.
- Risks associated with the external contracting itself.

The prospective provider should be asked for:

- Its description of the nature of each risk.
- The containment put in place.

Select provider and award the contract

- The contingency allocated along with the method of calculation for the associated risk budget.

It should be made clear who manages each risk as a contractual obligation and who has liability, i.e. if the risk happens then does the provider bear the resulting cost even if it has underestimated? There are two commonly occurring connected dangers here:

1. There may be confusion between management of the risk (who manages it) and liability if it happens. Ideally, they have the same owner, but not always.
2. Ownership, as expressed in the risk register, may conflict with its allocation in the conditions of contract.

Both 1 and 2 allow potential for dispute, therefore clear and unambiguous expression is vital.

In addition to the risks, prospective providers should indicate all dependencies upon which their proposals are based. These dependencies may result in additional risks in the employer's overall risk register.

Appendix A (Table A1) provides examples of the typical risks that are associated with external contracting together with containment/preventative measures that may be applicable and that should be accounted for during the selection process.

To avoid potential contractual commitments, all documents supplied during the selection process, including any meeting minutes, should include an appropriate declaration such as:

> *'The content of this document shall not constitute a contract either in part or in full and it shall not be implied that any contract is to be placed between any parties as a result of any statements herein', often shortened to 'without prejudice and subject to contract'.*[52]

6.3 Inputs

The inputs to the select provider and award the contract stage are:

---

[58] Broome, J. C. and Horne, R. 'Point of Law', pages 56–58, *Project* journal, issue 287, Summer 2016.

APM Guide to Contracts and Procurement

- The availability of the project sponsor and, if appointed, project board or steering group. Note that ownership of the selection process will be assigned as a first activity of the stage, including the appointment of a provider selection panel (PSP) for significant packages, where warranted.
- The business case and the procurement management plan documents. A briefing for the selection team (being an individual or PSP) should be prepared by the project sponsor focussing on issues relevant to the package but also of the wider project context. This briefing also needs to cover the available budget for the selection process (see section 3.4). Note that this briefing may give rise to some questions. For instance, if a cost-based contract strategy is specified, then ability to do 'open book' financial administration is a prerequisite for successful implementation. Not all providers may be prepared or able to do this.
- Knowledge, and in some cases expertise, on the relevant law. While this varies with geography, it generally follows similar principles. For each part of the world the appropriate research needs to be done to determine the compliance requirements. In the case of procurement crossing national boundaries, the jurisdiction applying needs to be specified. As an example, while the EU Procurement Directive covers the EU member states and applies to all bodies doing work for public authorities; it is enacted in the UK by an Act of Parliament and therefore will continue to apply until this Act is changed, even after the UK has formally left the EU. This legislation specifies criteria and process including the need for, format and content of an advertisement right at the outset of the process. If you wish to change something that was stated in the original advert, then the competition has to start again. Such legislation is subject to change and case law, so is not covered in detail here, but can be found on up to date websites. Note that although precise EU procedures apply to only public sector work the principles of fair competition law[53, 54] apply to all contracting work, of whatever value and also between private sector providers. In competitive tendering the contracting process must be manifestly fair to all.
- The requirement as the nature of the work and ball park monetary value will largely determine to whom the potential package is advertised and which tenderers it will attract.

[53] UK Act of Parliament, 1998, The Competition Act 1998.
[54] Act of Parliament, 2002, The Enterprise Act 2002.

Select provider and award the contract

- By the time of the final selection, in most competitions, it will be necessary to have the final draft contract terms, requirement and form of pricing document (albeit not yet priced) in place prior to the final round of the competition as this will dictate the prices tendered, including risk allowances, as well as written responses which are specific to the package.

6.4 Activities

The process is illustrated in Figure 6.1.

6.4.1 Activity 1: Appoint provider selection panel (PSP)

The PSP should include:

- Members from the project board or steering group.
- Those team members who are going to work with the provider (they could also be in the team who will do the administration and scoring).
- A representative of the ultimate user.

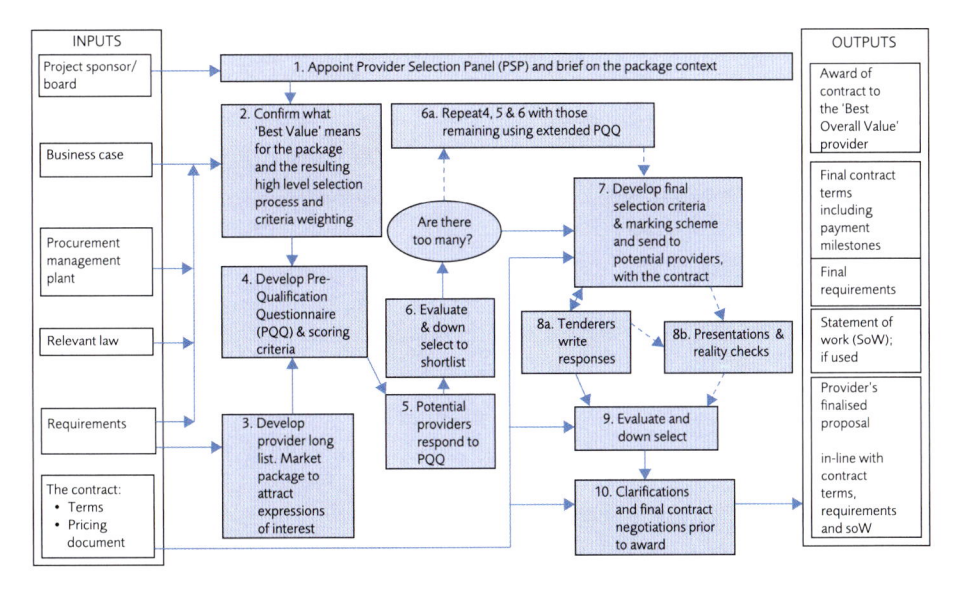

Figure 6.1 Process diagram for the provider selection stage

The PSP should be made up of unbiased personnel and the PSP members should be required to state any potentially biasing interest (e.g. share ownership in respondent companies or their parent companies). Any conflicts of interests should be declared very early in the tender process and where possible, such people should be replaced.

The PSP will typically have its own terms of reference (ToR), will set the ToR for the selection team and have an assigned chairperson.

6.4.2 Activity 2: Agree what 'best value' means for the package and resulting high level selection process, criteria and weighting

The first thing for the PSP to agree on is what process will be used to select the individual provider. The selection team may contribute further information affecting the budget. If so, then this should go through due governance and be approved or rejected by the project sponsor.

Table 6.1 gives a very brief overview of the four main procurement methodologies and, if they apply to the employer, the relevant EU procurement procedures.

Having decided on the most appropriate process, a programme of action needs to be drawn up which fits in with the overall project timescales. Where there are numerous packages to be tendered, then a 'tender event schedule' can be useful detailing all the pre-contract activities and ensuring that all can be achieved/resourced appropriately. Under EU procurement law, there are strict minimum timescales which have to be adhered to. Given this, it is sensible to have the initial meeting of the PSP sooner rather than later.

For most selections, there are two stages. Prior to getting into the detail of writing questions, a set of outline selection criteria should be established, which can then be developed by the selection team, prior to being signed off by the PSP.

The initial shortlisting criteria will form the basis for the pre-qualification questionnaire (PQQ). They should be short and simple to answer, both by the organisations that might respond and those who will score them. As an example, a criterion could be that any company has to have a turnover of at least four times the estimated value of the contract. This is so that any competing organisations can quickly de-select themselves and not waste time on bids that they cannot win. Likewise, the scoring organisation will not then have to spend time evaluating what turn out to be non-compliant organisations. It should be noted that when compiling a PQQ there are potentially mandatory PQQ criteria to include, linked to the regulation requirements applying (see section 6.0 above).

Criteria for the final selection, when there are fewer competing organisations, tend to be more subjective and therefore take longer both to write and score. The exception to this is the price component, which is easy to score. We suggest (and this method is commonly used) that a weighted value tree is used to understand what is important to the employer or project for this selection exercise. This should be broken down into more detailed criteria around which questions can be based and the answers weighted in proportion to the importance the employer attaches to them. An example is given in Figure 6.2.

Table 6.1 provides advice of when to use a particular selection methodology against the type of work being procured.

6.4.3 Activity 3: Develop the provider long list

The provider long list (if required, depending on the procurement route) is compiled following research of the available providers. The idea is to 'market' the package to attract expressions of interest. This can be undertaken via Internet search engines, industry periodicals, buying guides, recommendations and previous experience. Consider hiring category/sector specialists, placing open adverts, hosting 'meet the buyer' events.

Market the package with the aim of ensuring that potential providers are not only aware that it is out there, but that the best and most capable (for the package) will bid, i.e. forming an attractive proposition to them. Key information, including an overall description of the outline requirements is a prerequisite, together with the likely timescales for delivery. Consider doing this far earlier in the process to have sufficient time to do it justice – compile a tender event schedule very early in the project process (strategy stage or concept stage – to avoid 11th hour work). If it is a major and unique package, industry 'open days' may be held to consult with those likely to bid. This helps shape and inform potential bidders how the package will be let and engages with those who will ultimately provide the package. A word of caution though; the engagement method will often determine the initial impression of the employer. If this impression is not good, then it can adversely affect the attractiveness of the package to the market and may damage the employer's reputation.

APM Guide to Contracts and Procurement

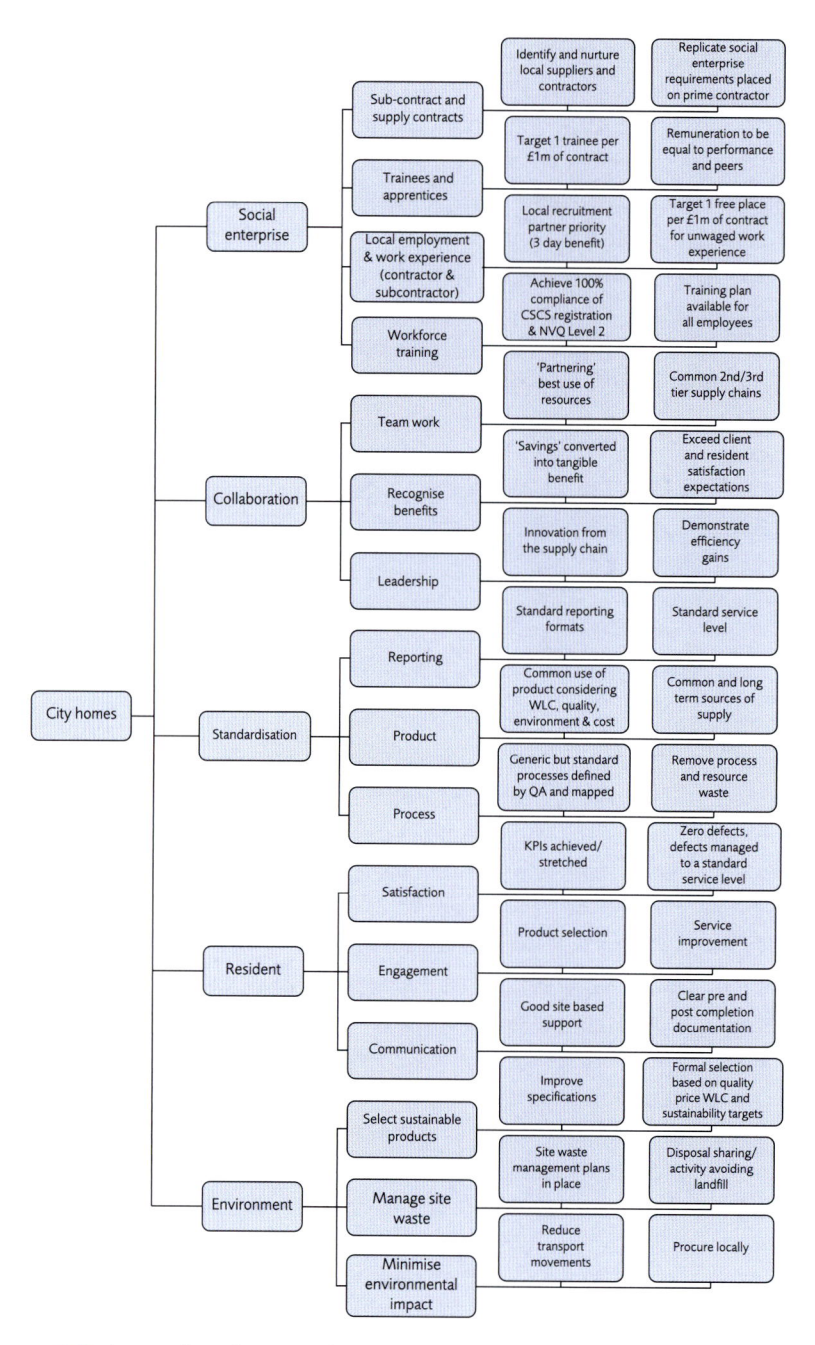

Figure 6.2 Example value tree for a housing association appointment

Table 6.1 Characteristics of differing procurement methodologies

Type	Characteristics	When to use (See also section 3.3.6 for consideration of the type of supplier relationship)	Equivalent EU procedure (2016 guidance)[55]
Open market (any organisation can respond)	Advertised to the world. Large number of bidders Selection on lowest price For example, e-Auctions.	When there is an exacting or precise specification, normally for goods, and a sufficient number of providers who can supply it (i.e. commodity type goods).	**The Open Procedure**
Limited competition (two stage)	When the employer has significant knowledge of the market place and past experience of individual providers (i.e. where an initial selection can be done based on experience). Initial stage using a PQQ, or only a short list invited to tender. The final selection is typically done on best value criteria (a combination of price and other factors).	When there is a large number of providers who could *potentially* meet the unique requirement, some filtering for the best ones is needed prior to a detailed bid. For the final bid, the employer can define what it is they want to a level of detail that ensures they will get it and the constraints that the bidder must adhere to, yet both of these give the bidder some leeway to innovate to give a 'best value' bid, howsoever that is defined.	**The Restricted Procedure** Note that there has to be a two-stage competition to be compliant. For 'best value' read 'most economically advantageous tender' (MEAT).
Ongoing discussion, then negotiation with a limited number of providers	Employer cannot define exactly what they want and/or how it is to be delivered. They use the market place to help them define this and, in doing so, the market better understands the requirement.	High value adding requirements with a large risk – both opportunity and threat – element in it.	**The Competitive Dialogue and Competitive Dialogue with Negotiation Procedures** A three-stage process of pre-qualification; invitation to participate in the dialogue; and invitation to tender (best and final offer).
Single source	Where the solution is very specific to a known source. Request for submission of alternative ideas by providers. Negotiation with new providers or single source.	When time or quality is paramount. Ideally, there is an ongoing commercial relationship which prevents the employer from being taken advantage of when pricing.	**The Innovative Partnership Procedure**

[55] Based on the UK Government Guide (UK Crown Commercial Service, 2016).

If the procurement is undertaken from within the EU and meets certain criteria,[56] then the employer will have to publish in 'Supplement S' of the *Official Journal of the European Union*,[57] which will attract interest from those who think that they can fulfil the outline requirement, i.e. the wider market itself may determine the long list. We suggest that further helpful information about the package be available to those potential bidders that may not know the particular application domain of the package.

6.4.4 Activity 4: Develop pre-qualification questionnaire (PQQ) and scoring criteria (and send to potential providers)

Once it is known how many and which providers are interested, a pre-qualification questionnaire can be written, together with scoring criteria.

The following information is normally asked from prospective bidders at this stage:

- **Financial information:** In order to provide reassurance that an organisation has the financial resources to deliver the package. For instance, current credit rating or the sales revenues of the organisation relative to the estimated value of the proposed package.
- **Industry and other external accreditations:** For example, in the aerospace sector providers may need to be accredited to specific aviation standards, or in their industries there may be specific BS/ISO standards to comply with. A common accreditation requirement in all sectors is accreditation to ISO9001, the generic international quality standard.
- **Organisational capacity and its capability to deliver the outline package:** This concerns the potential provider's track record of successfully delivering similar packages.

The reviewing of the presented financial information and accreditations will normally yield a 'yes/no', 'pass/fail' result. The associated thresholds need to be clearly stated in the PQQ to allow competing providers to quickly de-select themselves and thus not waste time on bids that they cannot win. Likewise, the

---

[56] See http://europa.eu/business/public-contracts/index_en.htm for further information.
[57] The *Official Journal of the European Union* (the *OJEU*) is the official gazette of record for the European Union (EU). It is published every working day in all of the official languages of the member states.

Select provider and award the contract

selection panel will not then have to spend time evaluating what turn out to be non-compliant bidders. Indeed, if subject to EU procurement legislation, potential providers are entitled to be informed of the criteria and thresholds at the time that the PQQ is issued.

See section 6.4.7 (Activity 7) below for advice on the development of the scoring criteria, which also applies to the PQQ version.

Regarding a presented track-record of successfully delivering similar projects, most providers will have libraries of 'case studies' which they will select and fine tune depending on the information they have on the employer, the package and the specific questions asked. A challenge (particularly when at this stage there may be a high number of responses to a PQQ) is to determine the veracity of the presented case studies, as often the material presented may be 'glossy marketing material'. Consequently, 'hard' and verifiable data and references need to be requested. As an example of 'hard' verifiable data, in the construction sector there is a scheme called the 'considerate constructor scheme' whereby, for each project, external assessors give a score on how well a provider has managed any impacts on neighbouring parties, including members of the public and any adjacent businesses.

We recommend that a number of words or page limit is set to encourage full, but succinct responses to the PQQ.

Questions asked in the PQQ should be posed from the perspective of what is required for the specific package; however, the bar needs to be set at an appropriate height to ensure that the market has the ability to supply it.

Too low a bar and/or too many 'yes/no' or 'pass/fail' type questions may lead to:

- Too many of the interested potential providers pre-qualifying for the next round.
- There being little to distinguish those most suitable and able from those less suitable and able.

In either of the above cases this may lead to the need for an unplanned extended PQQ (Activity 6a) to be inserted into the process, which causes extra expense and time to the employer, as well as the potential providers.

On the other hand, too high a bar will lead to an absence of sufficient competition at the final selection stages. To avoid an overly labour intensive final stage of selection we recommend that the number of bidders for that stage be targeted to be between three and six.

In some cases, it may not be necessary to run an external pre-qualification competition at all. Knowledge, research and effective marketing may mean that the employer's selection panel may identify a sufficient number of suitable and creditable potential providers to move to the final selection process without the need for a pre-qualification competition (with due regard to fairness of competition law). This can save all parties concerned the associated time and cost.

6.4.5 Activity 5: Potential providers respond to the PQQ

Observing the guidelines as expressed in Activity 4 above should minimise the cost and time required to respond to a PQQ. Nevertheless, prospective providers will need to allocate due time and resources to respond within the timescales required. It is therefore important to provide prior warning of there being a pending PQQ in order that providers can appropriately plan bidding activities.

Be clear regarding how potential providers should respond in terms of the medium (e.g. hard copy, e-tender tool or email), where the response should be sent and, of course, a closure deadline. Also, state in the documentation that the employer:

- reserves the right not to place any contractual arrangement following the PQQ evaluation;
- will not be responsible for any work undertaken by responding organisation or costs involved, and
- may require further stages of selection.

This information should all be defined in the PQQ pack together with how to communicate with the employer regarding any questions and queries.

6.4.6 Activity 6: Evaluate and down select to a shortlist

During this activity, the responders to the PQQ are evaluated and marked against the assigned scoring criteria. If the previous stages have been well executed (in terms of the questions posed in the PQQ and the scoring criteria) then the process should not be too onerous in terms of scoring each individual response.

It, however, remains a risk that if the package has been successfully marketed and the bar set too low, then marking the resulting high number of responses can be quite an onerous activity. Regardless, the selection process against PQQ

Select provider and award the contract

responses should generate a shortlist of between three and six potential providers. Both the successful and unsuccessful responding organisations should be informed of their selection/non-selection at this stage. If you give any reasons for their non-inclusion make sure it is short, succinct and based on fact. It is best in the long run to be honest with the reasoning given.

6.4.6.1 Activity 6a: Repeat 4, 5 and 6 with those remaining using an extended qualification questionnaire (EQQ) if there are too many

In highly competitive markets it is sometimes difficult to select a shortlist immediately from consideration of the PQQ responses. This could be by design, whereby the initial PQQ is more designed to quickly eliminate those definitely *not* suitable, while the EQQ is designed to go a bit deeper to select those *most* suitable. Alternatively, it could be by accident whereby the initial PQQ did not provide sufficient differentiation for the final selection. For example, in extreme circumstances, say *15 organisations* scored top marks, in this case an EQQ is used to request further information to be considered.

6.4.7 Activity 7: Develop the final selection criteria and marking scheme and send tender to potential providers, together with a draft contract

To ensure fairness and a 'level playing field', key information that has a bearing on the requirements must be provided to all contenders. This information often is generated as the response to questions asked by potential providers, but which clarifies the solution required for all. The requirements for the solution may also have changed during this dialogue (e.g. an off-the-shelf solution may be found that eliminates custom works), and in that case all contenders should be informed of the change.

If Activity 2 has been carried out thoroughly then the selection team will have a good basis for developing the final selection criteria. The final selection criteria will need to take account of further technical detail that will have been developed in parallel with the PQQ process and also may be influenced by specific responses to the PQQ/EQQ. Such feedback from potential providers may point to the most efficient implementation methodology. The score weighting will then need to be updated in consultation with the PSP for sign-off.

APM Guide to Contracts and Procurement

The most common error we observe when developing scoring criteria is that they are expressed in too prescriptive a way, almost telling the potential providers what to write in their responses. This can lead to there being little or no differentiation between responses. This is particularly irksome at the top of the scoring criteria when one potential provider just 'ticks the boxes' to score maximum marks, while another does this and manages to differentiate themselves with the 'wow' factor, yet also scores the same top marks. An example scoring criteria which may avoid this pitfall is given in Table 6.2.

Make sure the scoring metrics are objective, relevant and specific – not too generic, and not too long as to make points irrelevant. Consider whether some scores are part of a weighted approach or are yes/no gates.

Good practice is that the final invitation to tender (ITT) includes the scoring criteria to be used and if subject to EU procurement legislation this is obligatory.

As outlined in Activity 4, we re-iterate the desirability of number-of-words or page-limiting written responses.

Table 6.2 Example scoring criteria

Score	Response Type	Reason indicated for Score
0	Non-compliant response	No relevant information/solution provided in response to contract requirements.
1	Unacceptable response	Partially compliant response but with serious deficiencies in solution offered, indicating serious difficulties/inability to deliver contract requirements.
2	Unsatisfactory response	Partially compliant response with shortfalls in solution offered, indicating not all contract requirements could be met and thus difficulty in delivery of the contract.
3	Acceptable response	Compliant response, indicating basic contract requirements are met but not exceeded. Contract could be delivered.
4	Good response	Compliant response, clearly indicating entire delivery can be met and solution offers some limited benefits beyond stated requirements.
5	Excellent response	Compliant response, bidder illustrated comprehensive understanding of contract reqs. Proposed solution provides significant additional benefits beyond stated reqs.

Select provider and award the contract

A full invitation to tender (ITT), which is issued to all tenderers, normally consists of:

- The instructions to tenderers which detail the process that is to be followed and relevant timescales. If there are to be presentations and reality checks, especially if scored, these should be stated up front. The instructions should include:
    - An introduction to the project explaining the overall outcomes expected, the scope of work, key specifications and overview drawings.
    - Any specific questions if the bidder is being requested to submit a technical proposal.
    - Details of any project constraints, such as the programme sequence or site access.
    - The form of pricing, which may be in a prescriptive form to allow comparison.
    - Details of any mid-tender meetings and/or questions and answers process.
    - A checklist for what documentation should be submitted with the tender (to ensure all required info is provided).
- An outline programme schedule indication.
- The (near final) draft contract pack (including contract terms, requirement, any annexes (e.g. a statement of work – see section 6.4.10.2 below) and pertinent standard reference documents applying.

Lastly, it is an option that potential providers may be given the opportunity to provide a non-compliant, or variant, bid in addition to the compliant bid. This gives the potential providers an opportunity to offer a 'value added' solution where the additional benefits (whether due to enhancements or cost savings) may outweigh those of the proposed technical requirement as given. This could include, for example, removing a constraint. The ITT should state how such a non-compliant proposal is to be evaluated.

6.4.8 Activity 8: Tendering provider proposals and interaction

The final ITT engagement process may consist of the provision of written responses and formalised clarification questions and answers or may additionally include presentations and 'reality checks'. The applicable process elements are described in Activities 8a and 8b below.

APM Guide to Contracts and Procurement

6.4.8.1 Activity 8a: Tenderers provide their responses

As with the issuing of a PQQ in Activity 5, reasonable prior notice of the issuing of the ITT should be given to the short-listed providers to enable the mobilisation of their bidding teams.

The potential provider's proposal-writing team will often need to include busy subject matter experts and also delivery personnel that may well have commitments to delivering existing already won work. Sufficient time must therefore be allowed for responses to be prepared.

6.4.8.2 Activity 8b: Presentations and reality checks

The process of assessment of individual ITT responses may often be helped by undertaking additional activities consisting of presentations and/or 'reality checks', as described below.

Presentations (or a project 'walk-through') to clarify understanding of what has been bid: It may be appropriate to request responders to give a time-limited presentation to the PSP followed by a question and answer session. The reasons for doing this include:

- standing back from the detail of the individual responses to gain the 'big picture' of what will be delivered and how it will be delivered;
- to clarify the detail of individual responses; and
- in doing the above, see 'the whites of the eyes' of the people that the employer's team will hopefully be working with, as opposed to against, to deliver the package successfully.
- During these interactions an assessment should be made of how much management time is likely to be needed to interact with the provider. This estimate should feed into the overall management budget for the project.

Consider the merit of doing this either before, during or after the bid, depending on timescales – to get a good mutual understanding it will be needed at some point, and possibly on multiple occasions. So allow enough time to do it.

Reality checks (a process to clarify the bids received): Reality checks can be undertaken to differentiate potential providers and to weed-out those that have made embellished claims. Forms of reality checking include:

Select provider and award the contract

- Demonstrations of existing similar solutions.
- Visits to existing customer sites, or other facilities (e.g. manufacturing) that the provider would use in implementing its proposed solution.
- Checking references, via telephone conference or more formal interviews.
- Observing the proposed provider team in action by, for instance, setting them a scenario for them to work through. Sometimes, this would include them working with the employer's team.
- Evaluating their behaviour when in negotiation.

For both the conducting of presentations and the undertaking of any reality checks the PSP may need to be augmented by the inclusion of key subject matter experts (SMEs) and the employer's delivery personnel to address the due technical detail and to assess the tenderer's responses to technical questions.

It should be noted that throughout both presentations and reality checking careful management is required to ensure that unfair bias does not creep in.

It should be emphasised that the same unbiased format should be used for all bidders. Beware lethargy. Allow sufficient time – you don't want to be rushing through meetings – this is the time to get the package understanding right.

Document the outcomes of the meeting, and follow the clarification up professionally. These clarifications can be used (and relied upon) later, as part of the final contract if carefully prepared.

6.4.9 Activity 9: Evaluate and down select

The evaluation and down-select process followed for the ITT must be consistent for all responders. Standard, let alone good, practice is that the scoring criteria is prepared prior to receiving responses:

- If subject to EU procurement, tenderers must know the scoring criteria prior to bidding.
- The more subjective the responses, i.e. written text, the more important it is to have a number of markers and to record reasons for the final mark, especially if there is initially variation in scoring, e.g. if initial scores range from 3 out of 10 to say 8 out of 10, with the final score being 7, the difference of opinion needs to be reconciled and justification for the final score. This is especially true under procurements subject to EU procurement regime, as to satisfy transparency, bidders can see these reasons and challenge.
- It makes sense to collate these scores and the weightings in a spreadsheet which calculates final mark automatically (see Table 6.3).

APM Guide to Contracts and Procurement

Table 6.3 Example provider selection scoring table

Item	Aspect Weighting	Element Weighting	Supplier 1	Supplier 2	Supplier 3	Supplier 4
Product Demonstration	10%		66%	90%	71%	63%
Demonstration 1		50%	62%	90%	70%	55%
Demonstration 2		50%	70%	91%	72%	70%
Functional Requirements	25%		84%	92%	74%	57%
Data Display		12%	65%	95%	65%	59%
Display Manipulation		12%	89%	98%	78%	50%
Tools		12%	88%	84%	51%	11%
Data Interfaces		12%	73%	93%	53%	10%
Standards Compliance		12%	84%	87%	82%	38%
Safety and Security		10%	83%	82%	87%	93%
Training		10%	85%	100%	57%	65%
Performance		10%	100%	100%	100%	100%
Host Platforms		10%	89%	88%	95%	90%
Technical Architecture	10%		77%	77%	70%	58%
Open Standard		40%	70%	70%	60%	50%
Service Orientation		40%	80%	80%	70%	50%
Ability to evolve with requirements		40%	80%	80%	80%	75%
Execution/Vision	20%		90%			
Vendor Viability		50%	90%	90%	90%	90%
Product Viability		50%	90%	90%	90%	90%
Indicative Cost	25%		72%	82%	38%	46%
Licence Structure		10%	90%	95%	80%	80%
Product Price		40%	94%	100%	13%	63%
Maintenance and Support Price		30%	45%	75%	0%	0%
Implementation Price		20%	60%	59%	60%	41%
Reference	10%		30%	70%	60%	60%
Reference Sites		50%	30%	70%	60%	60%
Customer Recommendations		50%	30%	70%	60%	60%
Overall Result			74%	67%	48%	44%

Select provider and award the contract

6.4.10 Activity 10: Clarifications and final contract negotiations prior to awarding the contract

Once the successful provider has been selected it is necessary to put in place the final agreed contract and arrangements for speedy start of the associated works.

6.4.10.1 *Final clarifications and negotiations*

In some cases, some further negotiation may be required to finalise the contract documentation. A good article which covers the common legal pitfalls and what to do about them can be found in the APM's *Project* magazine,[58] with an extended version published on-line.[59]

At this stage, it is important to ensure that the final contract documentation does not unfairly favour the selected tenderer over the other respondents. Any changes must not affect the result of tender evaluation (scoring). Additionally, it is imperative to check that the selected tenderer has responded against the latest and complete versions of the contract documentation with no amendments or questions outstanding.

6.4.10.2 *Contractual documents and associated content*

Ambiguity and precedence

The contractual documentation pack needs to be thoroughly checked to remove ambiguity, however there is a risk that some statements may be open to interpretation. For this reason, it is important to include a *statement of precedence* for the documents forming the pack. Providing numerous annexes can be useful but also can give rise to contention, therefore it is best to moderate the need for additional documents.

---

[58] Broome, J. C. and Horne, R. 'Point of Law', pages 56–58, *Project* journal, issue 287, Summer 2016.
[59] http://www.jonbroome.com/blog/june-2016/what-every-project-manager-should-know-about-offer and acceptance: common pitfalls of the ignorant and what to do about them.

Contract terms

The employer will provide the terms that define the contract, which will be nominally as defined in the prepare contract terms and requirement stage (see Chapter 4), but may require adjusting following the negotiations undertaken during provider selection. The 'conditions' of contract form the top-level document that will define the legal basis for the contract and will normally be drafted by the employer's commercial department or lawyer. Conditions are the words that cannot change except by a supplementary agreement by the parties to the contract. Other documents and terms, such as the requirement, may be in 'bite sized' annexes. This allows for flexibility during the negotiation phase and during execution, when it may be appropriate to apply contract changes. Annexes may also refer to additional documents (e.g. a SoW).

The provider's technical proposal (if applicable)

For performance type specifications, the provider may also have had to develop a technical proposal response (to varying levels of detail) which details what the provider is going to supply to satisfy the employer's performance requirements. If one of the principal reasons for selecting the provider was because of the advantages of their proposed technical solution this document may be referenced as an annex in the contract. If not, at best, there will be arguments which, at worst, may result in the provider not having to supply the technical solution which was a primary reason for their selection (although they would still have the legal obligation to meet the employer's requirements).

In addition to referencing the document into the contract, we also recommend that there is an explicit statement in the conditions giving precedence (see *ambiguity and precedence* above) to the employer's performance requirements. This is to ensure that if there is an ambiguity or inconsistency between the two documents, then the employer's requirements will prevail.

A statement of work (SoW)

A SoW can be a useful tool as an annex to the contract terms to provide specific details for the solution not contained in the requirement and for example, the preferred project management methodology. The SoW may allow iterative dialogue, regarding specific points, to go on as parallel negotiations to define the optimal way for *how* the solution is to be delivered by the provider.

Beware however, that a SoW can also be a further source of interpretation and ambiguity and therefore an ongoing review needs to be carried out across all contractual documents. As stated above, we recommend that a precedence clause is included mandating the precedence tree.

The SoW may go through a series of drafts to clarify work packages and procedures. Example content may include (**if not already covered in the contract terms or requirement**):

- Description and scope of work.
- Expected key milestones.
- Deliverables list and acceptance criteria.
- Quality requirements.
- Project management requirements (e.g. risk management, organisation chart, key meetings).
- Communications provisions.
- Security requirements.

6.4.10.3 Provider's priced proposal

The provider should respond against the documentation pack in the form of its cross-referenced priced proposal. The response may be split into 'technical' and 'commercial (priced quotation)' bindings for consideration by separate employer departments. As above it needs to be stated and understood that in the case of any contention remaining (which should have been eliminated) then the employer's documentation will take precedence.

Once the parties are ready to enter into a contract, the provider should acknowledge its acceptance and this is most conveniently facilitated by the employer sending an acceptance form or 'form of agreement' with the contract documents for signing and return. Make sure that any changes/clarifications are embodied in the contract terms *now*, and not left until after the contract is signed.

Some special contracts, such as deeds, are different from normal contracts. It should be considered whether part of the contract being considered may involve a deed or another special contract to be required (e.g. a deed will govern a conveyance of land or interests in land, certain types of mortgage or charge, powers of attorney). In these circumstances a lawyer should be consulted to look at the specifics and the bearing on any other contract.

6.5 Outputs

6.5.1 Award of contract

Once the successful provider has been selected the award of contract is enacted by the contract being signed by authorised parties representing the provider and the employer. Note that these parties need to hold the appropriate delegated authority level for the value of the contract. It also needs to be double-checked that the provider has signed the contract based on the full set of finally agreed documents supplied by the employer and has not made any amendments.

7

Manage and deliver the contract

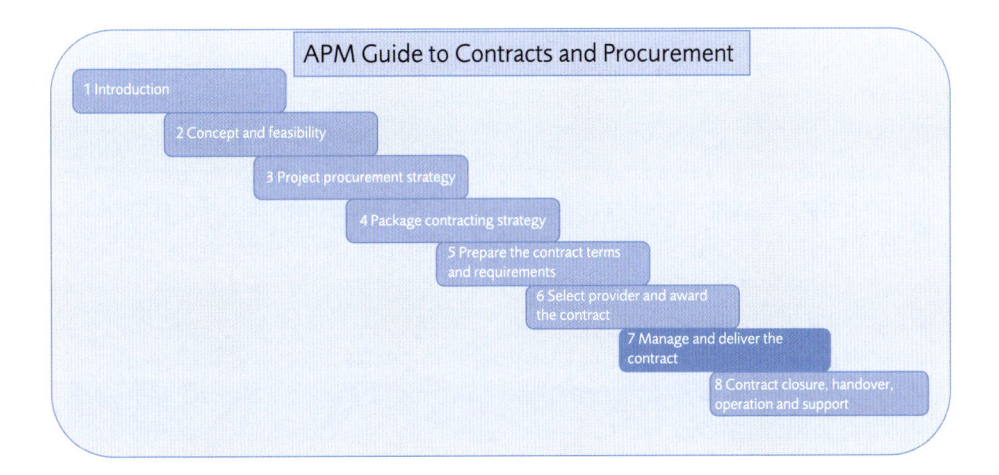

APM Guide to Contracts and Procurement
1 Introduction
2 Concept and feasibility
3 Project procurement strategy
4 Package contracting strategy
5 Prepare the contract terms and requirements
6 Select provider and award the contract
7 Manage and deliver the contract
8 Contract closure, handover, operation and support

7.0 Overview

This chapter describes the delivery stage; when the employer's project manager is required to manage the delivery of what has been described in the individual providers' contract(s) as part of the overall project. The employer's project manager will have initiated the overall project and briefed his/her internal team as part of the organisation's standard project management procedures. Management and delivery of the contract therefore is a flow-down of that process in the context of using an external provider. The delivery process described below is for a significant contract. The process should be tailored to be cost effective in keeping with the cost-base for the contract. The individual management budget should have been determined during the select provider and award the contract stage (see section 6.4.8.2).

7.1 Background

Once the contract has been placed 'and the clock is ticking' the provider is obliged to deliver the required solution in keeping with the specific provisions of the contract.

Solution delivery is best broken down into manageable chunks (or phases) as shown in Figure 7.1 although it should be recognised that these phases may often overlap and involve repetition to iteratively build-up the solution over time.

To re-iterate a point we made earlier, it is necessary that the employer's project/contract manager has the ability to manage the contract as well as administrating it. By 'administrating' the contract, we mean, for example, certifying payment and ensuring technical compliance against progress in stages. Traditionally, 'administrating' has also meant collecting records in order to be able to defend a potential payment claim once the full requirement has been delivered.

During drafting of the contract terms, flexibility to allow the efficient management of change should have been addressed. The contract should not tie the hands of the employer's project manager to be able to apply flexibility where it is due and as the project progresses. Such flexibility can often avoid undue negotiation dialogue that has to be backed-up by the associated paperwork. Of course a project manager may be assigned following the completion of all of the previous stages. In this case the project manager may find encumbrances that are not ideal, such as an inadequate provider selection process. In this case the project manager may need to backtrack to revisit the earlier processes (using this guide as an aid) to make-good the situation. The generic procurement and contracting risks of Appendix A may also provide a useful checklist to spot emerging issues.

7.2 Inputs

The inputs to the manage and deliver the contract phase will be formed by the outputs of the previous stages, including as a minimum:

- Written acceptance of the contract from the provider signed by a duly authorised person (checked to ensure that the version is the latest and is not subject to modification).
- The conditions of contract document.
- The requirement document.
- All other documents referenced in the contract, including where applicable:

Manage and deliver the contract

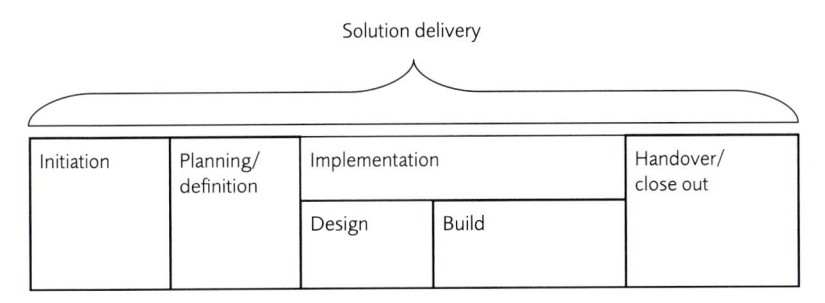

Figure 7.1 Solution delivery phases

- Statement of work.
- Non-disclosure agreement (NDA).
- Work breakdown structure.
- Project schedule.
- Key payment milestone and acceptance criteria definition.
- List of deliverables.
- List of dependencies and assumptions.
- Risk register.
- Security requirements.
- Warranty and support provisions.
- The provider's technical proposal.
- The provider's pricing document.

It should be noted that some, if not all, of these documents may be commercially sensitive and the appropriate marking should be applied according to the non-disclosure agreement (e.g. 'commercial in confidence' quoting the NDA reference). Due attention must be paid to the personnel allowed to view this information, e.g. where more than one provider is used each may be mutually excluded from viewing the other's documents.

7.3 Activities

The overall process is illustrated in Figure 7.2 and the individual activities are described below.

At the outset, the initiation stage sets up the necessary infrastructure for running the overall project and should include forming the necessary relationship(s) with the provider(s).

APM Guide to Contracts and Procurement

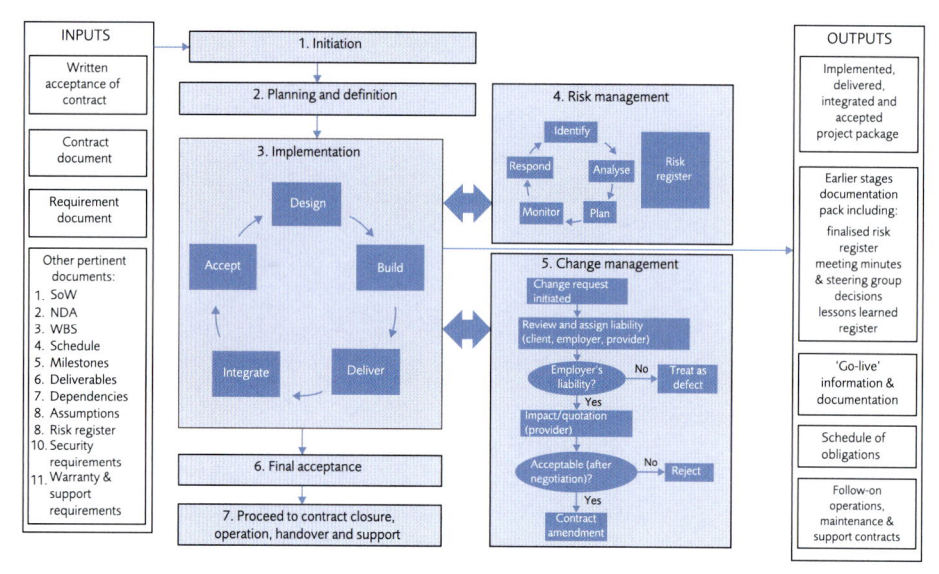

Figure 7.2 Manage and deliver the contract process

It is almost inevitable that some more detailed delivery planning will need to be conducted to firm-up the detail of what the provider(s) need to supply and how it will integrate with the rest of the solution; including the employer's work packages and those of any other providers. The planning/definition stage is therefore included following Initiation, its depth depending on the level of planning already conducted during provider selection.

The follow-on implementation stage may include design and build sections, culminating in the final delivery of the solution preceding the contract closure, handover, operation and support stage (see Chapter 8). For goods, the delivery of the requirement may be at a point in time. For works, such as the construction of an asset, delivery happens over a period of time.

Several parallel management activity streams need to be carried-out during Implementation:

- **Work package execution (whether internal or contracted):** The work must be undertaken in an ordered sequence to take account of the dependencies across the delivery teams. This often is carried out in a cyclic fashion to allow for integration of the work package outputs to take place to build up the solution.
- **Risk management:** Risks may emerge, become issues or be retired throughout implementation and need to be constantly managed to minimise impacts.

- **Change control:** Changes during implementation (whether initiated from internal or external sources) are to be expected and need to be catered for as part of the normal delivery process. Depending on the risk allocation in the contract, some change will be at the provider's risk and some will be at the employer's risk resulting in a price change and/or schedule extension.

7.3.1 Activity 1: Initiation

Initiation needs to focus on the specific needs of the contracting relationship for each individual package (large projects may need several initiation streams covering many packages). Regardless, it needs to be done quickly and efficiently and in accordance with the contract – so before a package is initiated, key participants need to have read the contract.

The initiation stage is the point when the employer's project manager needs to take the initiative and provide leadership to his internal team and to the provider's project manager and senior team, promoting action and efficiency. We suggest that the employer's project manager uses a structured initiation process as described below in Figure 7.3.

7.3.1.1 Contract review

A first action of the employer's project management team should be to review the contract, specifically to ensure the contractual documentation (contract terms, requirement and any referenced SoWs) are correct and complete (particularly the issue status). Inconsistencies or omissions could, in extremis, invalidate the contract. More likely, they will cause delay and extra cost to one or both parties, but aggravation for both parties. Moreover, the delivery team need to understand and appreciate how to operate the contract and what has to be delivered. The initiation phase (and indeed the follow-on phases) is eased significantly by the definition of detailed provider SoWs (annexed to the contract) during the select provider and award the contract stage (see Chapter 6).

7.3.1.2 Identify key roles, responsibilities and levels of delegation

Ideally – and highly desirable – is that the employer's project manager will have been involved during the negotiations and already have met the key players. Management of providers is very much a people-orientated activity and it is

APM Guide to Contracts and Procurement

```
┌─────────────────┐
│ Contract review │
│(internal employer│
│   PM activity)  │
└────────┬────────┘
         ↓
    ┌─────────────────┐
    │Identify key roles,│
    │ responsibilities and│
    │ levels of delegation│
    └────────┬────────┘
             ↓
         ┌─────────────────┐
         │Schedule meetings│
         │ and set agendas │
         │ (prioritising the│
         │provider inaugural or│
         │ kick-off meeting)│
         └────────┬────────┘
                  ↓
              ┌─────────────┐
              │  Formalise  │
              │communications│
              └──────┬──────┘
                     ↓
                 ┌─────────────┐
                 │ Agree tools,│
                 │conventions and│
                 │techniques to be│
                 │   adopted   │
                 └─────────────┘
```

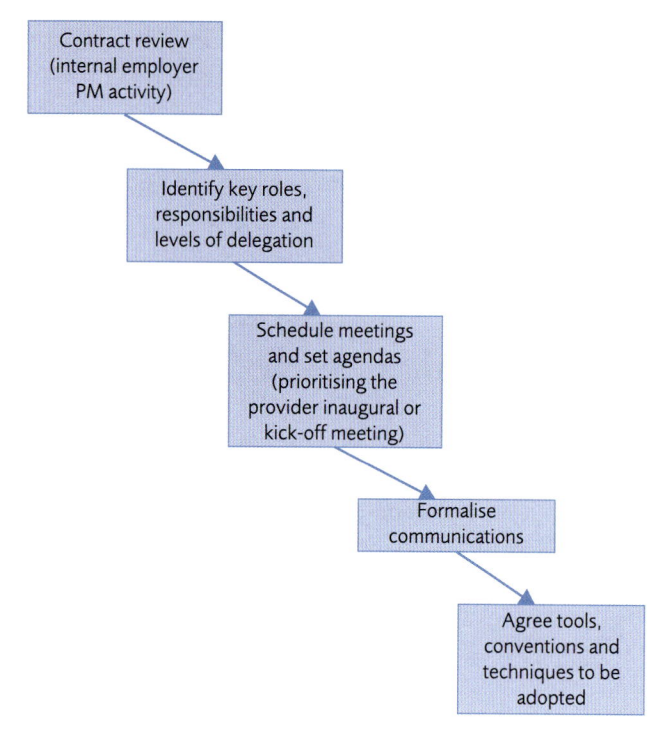

Figure 7.3 Initiation stages

desirable that people from all parties need to get to know each other (ideally during the negotiation phase but certainly at the inaugural meeting).

Responsibilities within the respective organisations should be defined so that ownership is clear. Stakeholders (all management staff including their names, seniority, responsibilities and reporting line – organisational chart) within each of the parties should be identified in order for the employer's project manager to develop a stakeholder management plan. Key roles are typically:

<u>For the employer</u>

Project manager: Oversees and has responsibility for the project delivery. Has ultimate responsibility for the performance of the project and providers.

Contract manager (if not the project manager): A person nominated to manage the provider, undertaking day-to-day communications and reporting progress and issues to the project manager.

Commercial/purchasing managers: Persons responsible for the contract and the drafting of any change orders.

Technical authority (TA): The senior person responsible for the technical solution.

Quality representative: The employer organisation's person responsible for approval of the quality plan, auditing and delivery quality sign-off.

For the provider

Project manager: The project manager responsible for all project management processes on the provider's behalf. This person will normally be the primary point-of-contact for the employer's project manager.

Commercial representative: The person responsible for contractual negotiations and pricing issues for the provider.

Technical authority (TA): The senior person at the provider responsible for the contracted technical solution.

Key design and development personnel: The team of personnel responsible for working on the contracted packages.

Quality representative: The person responsible for quality aspects on behalf of the provider.

Delegated authorities to perform key tasks (e.g. issuing/approving variations, signing off payments, etc.) should be discussed and agreed so that people know who their opposite number is and the limits of their authority. This delegation must be formally communicated across the parties.

7.3.1.3 Schedule meetings and set agendas (prioritising the inaugural kick-off meeting):

The number and types of meetings, together with agendas should have been specified in the contract as this has a bearing on employer/provider costs. If not, then this needs to be specified. Regardless, details need to be worked through. The types of meeting normally consist of:

- A provider inaugural kick-off meeting.
- Regular review meetings.
- Technical meetings (e.g. design or gate reviews).
- Ad-hoc meetings to address specific concerns or issues.

For each type of meeting the nominal attendance, agenda and minutes format (and who takes them) needs to be set. Record keeping is vital to avoid different recollections of verbal agreements developing.

Provider inaugural kick-off (KO) meeting

It is good practice to invite representatives of the wider provider delivery team to the inaugural KO meeting to allow any questions or clarifications to be dealt

APM Guide to Contracts and Procurement

with. Where there are provider interdependencies then representatives of the involved providers should attend.

The KO meeting is a chance for the employer's project manager to assert his/her authority and make clear expectations. The KO meeting should be a platform to make sure all understand the drivers behind the project; what their part is in it and how the contract impacts on them. It is also a chance to gauge the 'atmosphere' and the temperament of the team members, which could impact performance. The employer's project manager should set the agenda and chair the meeting. A typical agenda would include:

- project/programme overview;
- stakeholder management;
- communications;
- change control;
- configuration management;
- quality management;
- planning and project schedule;
- reporting;
- resource planning;
- delivery planning;
- acceptance; and
- actions agreed.

The detailed governance arrangements for the employer and the provider need to be confirmed (in conformance with the contract), including an escalation procedure to cover how any issues/disputes that develop between the parties will be managed.

In section 4.4.5 we describe a formal set of *issue/dispute resolution procedures* which can form part of the contract in order to make clear the escalation process and the options in the event of a dispute becoming serious. By careful monitoring of the project's progress and the way in which the employer/provider relationship is progressing, the respective project managers can detect early warning of issue escalation enabling action to 'nip-in-the-bud'. A positive relationship formed between the respective employer and provider project managers is key to avoidance of costly issue escalation and potential litigation.

At the KO meeting points of contact (for inclusion in the communications plan) should be identified to allow the controlled transfer of information and day-to-day management interaction.

7.3.1.4 Formalise communications

In section 6.1.4 of the select provider and award the contract stage, we emphasise the importance of controlled communications. A communications plan should be developed to formalise communication routes and information management. The key roles, responsibilities and levels of delegation determined in section 7.3.1.2 should form the starting point and a RACI (responsible, accountable, consulted, informed) matrix developed (if not already specified in the contract) to identify who is responsible, accountable, consulted and informed during the contract.

7.3.1.5 Agree tools and conventions to be adopted

Different organisations will have chosen, or developed, their specific tools to be used to conduct their operations (registers, databases, workflow systems etc.). The tools chosen may impact the extent of information available and how it can be communicated to others (e.g. there are multiple project scheduling tools available – some compatible and others not). The contract may have specified the use of specific tools by the provider in which case there should be no issues. In many cases, it will be unrealistic to expect the provider to invest in specific tools to be compatible with the employer (e.g. the provider may have a large infrastructure that is costly to adapt, e.g. an electronics production line or material requirements planning (MRP) system).

It is necessary to determine the actual tools that will be used by each party and, if incompatible, how information will be transferred. Additionally, the conventions that will be used (e.g. date, time and document configuration standards).

Often, providing document performas (e.g. for the write-up of meetings and contractual communications between the parties) can help.

7.3.2 Activity 2: Planning and definition

It is unlikely that everything down to the last detail of exact goods and services will have been specified in the requirement. A planning and definition phase is therefore almost certainly required. Thorough planning often pays back hugely by saving wasted effort/rework during design/build.

Consultation: The key to a successful planning and definition phase is thorough consultation across all parties. Feedback from the provider should be thoroughly analysed as often suggestions from the implementer provide a practical/experienced insight into the problem areas and any 'stock' solutions available.

Technical agreement can often be expedited by undertaking workshops at which all contributing parties participate and have the chance to air their opinions/preferences. At such events, it is essential to state the objectives of the event and to ensure that it has a facilitator/chairperson. The outcomes in the form of decisions and actions should be carefully minuted to avoid subsequent contention.

Procurement-scheduling: An important planning activity is the linkage of the overall project schedule to the in-feeds required from the providers. Ideally in-feed dependencies have been taken into account during contractual negotiations. However, we find that in practice it is often the unexpected dependencies that cause cost and time overruns. Planning and definition activities therefore need to include a review of the respective schedules to identify any additional linkages (bearing in mind that manufacturing lead-times can vary day-to-day). Dependencies may also be due to the supplying of key information and approval turn-around. Bear in mind that there may also be provider–provider dependencies that could ultimately cause delay or cost overruns.

De-risking: During the planning and definition phase it is often of value to undertake investigative or experimental works in parallel with the above activities. Such activities may be able to reduce or remove risks that would otherwise impact the implementation phase. Examples of such activities would be to evaluate a number of competing products to make a selection or to produce a basic prototype/model to establish key performance parameters possible.

Planning and definition phase outputs: Typical outputs defined at the conclusion of the planning and definition phase include:

- documentation plan (indicating the hierarchy and ownership (provider/employer) of technical design documents);
- outcome of any de-risking activities;
- baseline provider schedule including project milestones in alignment with the payment milestones of the contract;
- updated risk management plan (for both parties); and
- approved quality plan.

These outputs should have been subject to review and any contention may trigger contract change requests, that should be resolved by the end of the planning and definition phase via the change control procedure (see section 7.3.5).

Manage and deliver the contract

7.3.3 Activity 3: Implementation

In Figure 7.2 we depict an 'implementation cycle': *'Design, Build, Deliver, Integrate, Accept'*. This is because the implementation; involving one or more providers as well as the activities of the employer's internal team is often cyclic in nature with individual packages being delivered throughout. Significant risk is introduced due to the need to integrate the works together, which may involve interdependencies between multiple contracted providers. Such interdependencies, which may be realised well into the overall project, are often cited as the most frequent cause of issues developing that can significantly impact time, cost and quality if not accounted for (see Appendix A).

The implementation cycle is affected by:

- The impact of realised risks and the resulting negotiations between parties to resolve the impact ownership (covered by the risk management activity – see section 7.3.4).
- The advent of necessary contract changes (covered by the change control process – see section 7.3.5). Changes may result from risk realisation, or from changes to the overall requirement.

During implementation, a good management technique for the employer's project manager to use is the Deming circle[60] (see Figure 7.4).

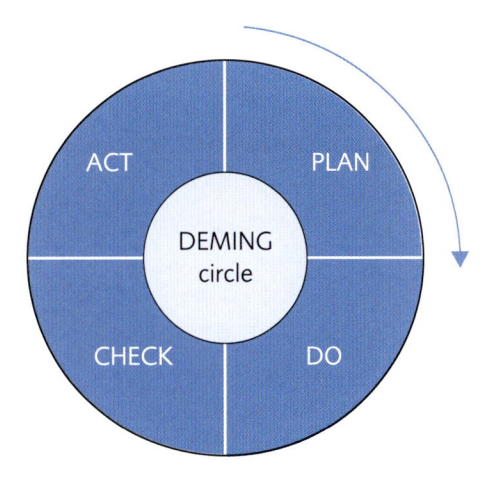

Figure 7.4 Deming circle

[60] Deming, E.D. *Out of the Crisis* (Deming, 1986).

APM Guide to Contracts and Procurement

The Plan, Do, Check, Act method can be used to evaluate overall status of the project and may be geared to the reporting cycle. It is essential to gain periodic performance and status information from the provider(s) via their respective project managers including, at least, the following aspects:

- Budget status.
- Schedule status.
- Earned value/cost-to-complete estimate (for input-based contracts).
- Key performance parameter status.
- Priorities and key objectives.
- Risk status.
- Issues status.
- Change request/approved change status.
- Status against plan/key milestones status.
- Exceptions and reason for incomplete/corrective action.
- Review of the contract closure/handover aspects (see Chapter 8).
- Next period plan.

Regular review and planning meetings should address all these items, but should mainly concentrate on any variances from plan or any issues arising and, importantly, what to do about them. Ideally, contractual risk allocation will be clear in the contract, so accountability for corrective action should be clear. Note that we have included a review of the handover (due at the end of the project) aspects in order to ensure these are considered during implementation rather than left until near the end. The frequency of progress reviews may not necessarily be constant through implementation but may increase at key times when a provider's delivery may be critical. 'More rather than less' communication is desirable. It can be difficult to get a complete assessment of the performance of off-shore providers and in this case a frequent (possibly even daily) 30-minute team teleconference can tease-out problems at an early stage.

A sufficient level of resources should be allocated for the review of the provider's design and deliverables. An appropriate technical understanding is necessary and, if not available internally, external consultants may need to be brought in to assist with reviews.

The 'build' sub-phase will include the ordering and expedition of any materials, inwards inspection, module fabrication and final assembly. In many cases the only way of properly monitoring the build sub-phase is by on-site inspection at the location where the work is being done. Such inspection may include:

- Checking of material orders placed.
- Checking of quantities of materials received and associated documentation (certificates of conformity, acceptance/test certificates, etc.).
- For off-shore providers, checking of import and export documentation and licences.
- Checking that provision has been made for storage, including space, environmental and safety provisions.

On-site fabrication, erection and installation works must be regularly monitored and earned-value analysis is often the best technique to use to understand the efficiency of the provider and to obtain a reliable prediction of *cost-at-completion* and the *completion-date* forecasts.

The cost of delays across the project may be amplified due to the unavailability of a provider's critical delivery. It is therefore vital to keep on top of progress; as liquidated damages clauses, if imposed, seldom will cover the resultant losses and damage to reputation. If slippage has occurred it may be the best policy to apply additional resources, possibly combined with incentivisation, to regain the schedule.

A factor to consider during the implementation phase and throughout the project generally, is the morale of workers, whether internal employees or provider's staff. An 'us and them' mentality can be quite damaging and can lead to poor performance. On a day-to-day basis, the employer's project manager should monitor morale and promote 'team spirit' throughout the greater team including the personnel at the provider's site. Team-building events such as get-togethers following attaining primary milestones may be worthwhile for lengthy projects; especially if there is an opportune moment when staff are co-located.

7.3.4 Activity 4: Risk management

When project packages are outplaced the risk management activity for the entire project or programme needs to be expanded to cover the associated risks. Additional risk aspects include:

1. The risk of using external contracted resources (Appendix A provides a list of the additional risks to consider).
2. Technical risks that are devolved to the provider, but that may none-the-less have impact on the time cost and quality of the main project or programme (the secondary effects).

APM Guide to Contracts and Procurement

7.3.5 Activity 5: Change control

> **Change control:** A process that ensures that all changes made to a project's baseline scope, cost, time or quality objectives are identified, evaluated, approved, rejected or deferred. *APM Body of Knowledge 6th edition*

When project packages are outsourced the management of changes is expanded to cover the potential provider contract changes that may be necessary.

Significant management time may be required to impact changes and determine whether provider contract(s) need to be changed. Figure 7.5 illustrates the basic change control process.

The change control process itself remains the same whether work is outsourced to providers or not. A change request may originate from the employer or the provider and will be recorded in the change log, as normal and evaluated by the employer's change control board. The difference for outsourced work is that there is a contract to be considered which will be a defining factor for costs.

Obtaining agreement on whether the detail of a particular requirement is actually a change to contract can often be a time-consuming process in itself,

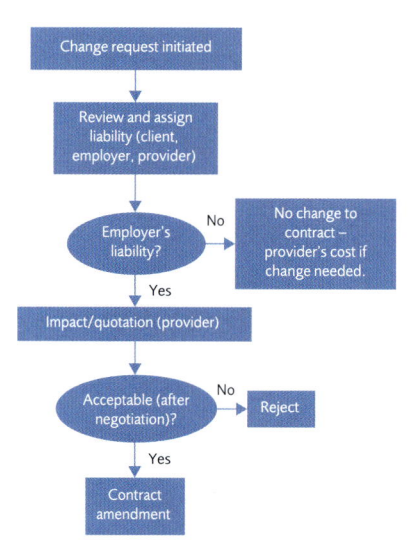

Figure 7.5 The change control process

154

particularly if there is room for interpretation of the contract documents. If it is determined that there is no actual change to contract then the provider is obliged to deliver accordingly. We strongly recommend the promotion of a degree of 'give and take' by both employer and provider (e.g. the detail of a particular requirement may be flexible without damaging the overall deliverables) to avoid lengthy negotiations and potential relationship damage. If it is determined that one or more provider contract(s) need to change then a negotiation needs to take place to quantify the cost of the change. This involves the provider(s) doing their own impact assessment and then quoting their price and timescale for effecting the change. Ideally, this conditions of contract give some structure and criteria for how the change is assessed. The change may be optional (e.g. an employer may ask the provider to quote for optional add-on to the work package) in which case if the provider's price(s) are not acceptable then the quotation(s) may be rejected. If the change is considered necessary then an unacceptable quotation from an existing provider may trigger a wider trawl covering potential new providers. Some cost-of-change containment factors when outsourcing project packages are:

1. During the package contracting strategy stage (see Chapter 4), provider inter-dependencies should be minimised; the more providers used, the higher is the risk that changes may affect multiple providers. Working with just one or two providers (by combining project packages) will contain the complexity of the change impacting task and associated costs.
2. The provider contract terms (see Chapter 5) should ensure that:
    a. The cost of bidding against contract changes is a liability of the provider.
    b. The provider's quoted price for the project package should include a reasonable and moderate amount of change without the need to re-quote (albeit any changes to the requirement will need to be fully documented).
    c. The employer reserves the right to seek competitive quotations against contract changes.
3. During the select provider and award the contract stage (see Chapter 6):
    a. Multiple sources for project packages should be identified, including the possibility of doing the work in-house. Back-up providers may need to be brought in should an existing provider's pricing be hiked to cover changes.
    b. Provider capacity should be established to check that a change does not prohibitively extend the schedule.
    c. At initial meetings, does it sound like any changes will be *'pounced-upon'* by a provider to make a significant increase to the price due to the initial 'buying of the job'?

The employer needs to be realistic in assessing the amount and quantum of likely change. Not only do they need to set aside a contingency for the amount which might be payable to the provider, they also need to sufficiently resource the contract with staff to not only manage the change (as in minimise likelihood and impact), but also administrate the contract to promptly agree the contractual change on time and cost. Our experience is that the longer this is put off because it is 'hard', then the harder it gets.

7.3.6 Activity 6: Final acceptance

7.3.6.1 Completion

Final acceptance may be the sign-off point for the provider to underpin its final claim for payment under the contract terms. This acceptance event usually follows integration of all the work packages to form the entire solution. Note that under some contractual schemes (e.g. BOOT and DBFO – see section 4.4.3) retention is also held by the employer pending a period of operation of the delivered solution (e.g. a performance bond).

During implementation, a number of phased integration events of different packages may have taken place (as indicated in Figure 7.2 activity 3). Employer and provider payment milestones may be attached to these interim events. At these interim events, it may be agreed that the work of some providers has been completed and their claims for full payment may be due. If this is the case, there will remain a risk that deviations and faults in their workmanship may emerge later in the project. The contract may already have anticipated this, specifying retention, bonds or parent company guarantees are kept in place until the asset has been up and running successfully for a period of time.

The final acceptance event (and any interim acceptance events) need to be documented by an acceptance certificate signed by the accepting authority (which may be an external party appointed by the ultimate employer). The acceptance certificate should document any defects and 'snagging' that need to be resolved before the assigned payment claim can be made. Note that it is best practice to ensure that the acceptance certificate is signed by the authorised parties at the acceptance event itself, rather than wait for it to be sent through or generated later.

The contract terms of any overarching contract of the employer may also include a guarantee period in which case this overarching guarantee needs to be flowed-down into the providers' contract terms.

7.3.6.2 Contract closure due to termination

Circumstances may have changed whereby a decision may have to be made over whether a project or a contracted package should continue or be terminated. This decision will invariably be based on an assessment on the project's continued benefits realisation as shown in Figure 7.6. Liabilities for terminating contracts need to be taken into account in deciding whether to terminate or not. For instance, under the contract, the employer may well not just have liabilities for the work done, but not yet paid for, but for costs committed by the provider and loss of profit.

Reasons for premature closure could be internal (e.g. performance issues) or external (e.g. due to the context of the overall project changing; company mergers, etc.).

If the project is still thought to be able to provide sufficient business benefits, then it should continue in its current or a similar configuration. If 'similar', then it might be that changes are made through the change control process (see section 7.3.5 above). If benefits are not at an appropriate level, then some other action will be required. This could include terminating the contract.

For instance, a project may have to provide for the maintenance of a company's owned car fleet. If the company decides to switch to a leased car system, then the maintained project is no longer required.

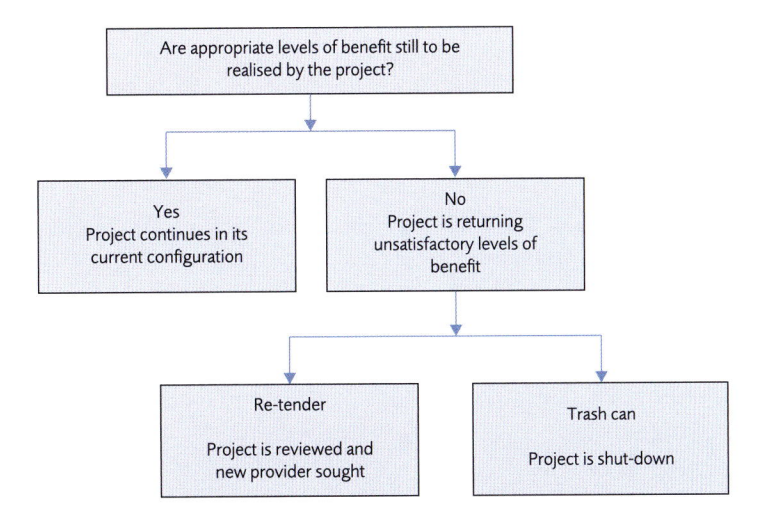

Figure 7.6 Contract closure decision

Ideally, the contract terms will give direction on how this is done and indicate the employer's liability, i.e. what will still be owed to the provider. It is very important that these mechanisms are followed otherwise the employer may end up paying significantly more than they would otherwise. If the mechanisms are not specified in the contract, then we recommend legal advice is taken in order to determine liabilities.

Once a decision is made to close a project down then the contract closure, handover, operation and support stage is entered, which is described in Chapter 8.

7.3.7 Activity 7: Follow-on contract closure, handover, operation and support (see Chapter 8)

Enabling contract closure, handover, operation and support is an essential part of the overall project delivery process (see Figure 7.2 activity 7) and is particularly important when significant works are outsourced to provider(s). Note that contract closure may have been required to occur early (see section 7.3.6.2).

Before signing a contract at the select provider and award the contract stage (see Chapter 6) the success criteria in the form of deliverables and performance should have been defined so that both the employer and provider have a shared understanding of what is to be delivered and how it is going to be accepted. These commitments should be jointly reviewed and understood. There may be a 'hands-off' contracting strategy, where the employer has minimal involvement during the majority of the delivery phase, however the handover to operations may still involve significant collaboration and joint planning.

7.4 Outputs

The outputs from the manage and deliver the contract stage will be a fully implemented, delivered, integrated and accepted project package as defined by:

- The contract documents defined above in the inputs section (see section 7.2).
- Any agreed modifications or additions to the contract documents that have been the subject of approved change notices.
- An updated documentation pack formed by the outputs of the earlier stages of the process including:
    - The business case, including the necessary project outcome, boundaries

Manage and deliver the contract

and scope (with particular emphasis on benefits realisation – including any benefits realisation plan produced).
  - ☐ The procurement management plan.
  - ☐ The archived provider selection documentation pack.
- Final project schedule that records the completion dates of the tasks.
- Finalised risk register that identifies any ongoing risks that have not been able to be retired.
- Archived meeting minutes.
- A record of steering group/project board decisions.
- 'Go-live' information (configuration information, back-up procedures, etc.).
- The documentation required for ongoing operations (including any user and installation manuals).
- A schedule of obligations that need to be fulfilled during ongoing operations, such as performance metrics and criteria that may be linked to a performance guarantee and against which funds are withheld.
- The follow-on maintenance, operation and support contracts.

8

Contract closure, handover, operation and support

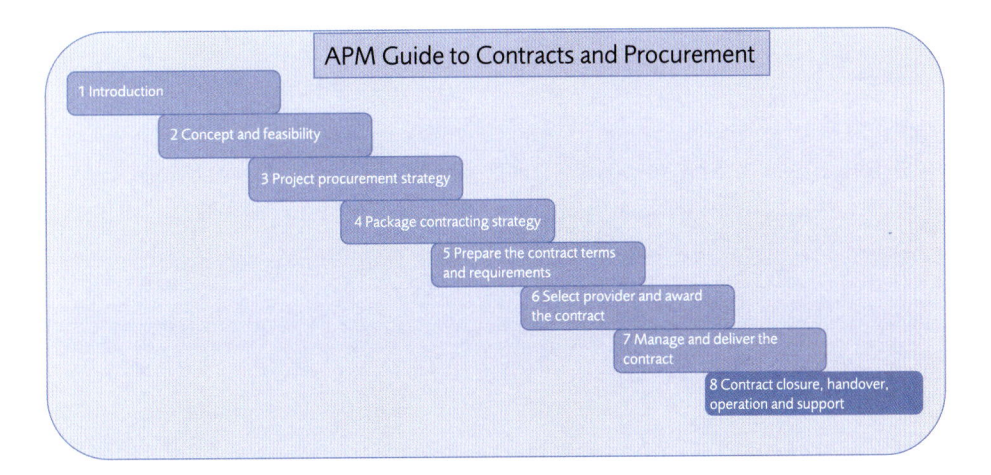

8.0 Overview

In this chapter, we consider the arrangements for contract closure, handover, operation and support defined as follows:

Contract closure: The completion of all activities associated with the delivery of a package including the supply of all necessary supporting information to the employer to enable closure and transit of the deliverables to the operational phase at handover.

> **Closure:** The formal end point of a project or programme, either because it has been completed or because it has been terminated early. *APM Body of Knowledge 6th edition*

Handover: The gate point at which the management and responsibility for the contract deliverables transfers from the provider's project package delivery team to the ongoing operational team (which may be the employer, the provider's operational team or a third party).

> **Handover:** The point in the life cycle where deliverables are handed over to the sponsor and users. *APM Body of Knowledge 6th edition*

Operation and support: The activities that follow-on from contract closure and handover, including the activities supporting ongoing operation and maintenance.

> **Operations management:** The management of those activities that create the core services or products provided by an organisation. *APM Body of Knowledge 6th edition*

8.1 Background

In most works contracts, on completion of delivery and acceptance, the tangible requirement will be handed back to the employer organisation to operate. From a contractual point of view, the common issues that need to be thought through and specified include:

- How the project is to be handed over to operations.
- Correction of any defects that emerge.
- Any ongoing service requirements.

Some general principles applying to contract closure, handover, operation and support need to be considered during the prepare contract terms and requirement stage (see Chapter 5), *before* the contract is signed.

- **Begin with the end in mind**: This should include pre-planning for:
    - Early termination.
    - Extended scope and the contractual conditions that must be met.
    - Any variation to the approach to liabilities that may apply.

- **Formulate your closure strategy:** Think about your closure strategy in sufficient time to plan it. This should include how you are going to ensure lower tier suppliers are achieving successful contract closure, without which you may not be able to achieve your top-level objectives. If you are the top level employer, you may wish to ensure that contract governance gives you assurance of the performance and costs of the whole supply chain to avoid last minute surprises due to issues between providers.
- **Determine the success criteria:** Make sure your success criteria are clear and unambiguous (as far as practicable) and ensure that incentives will drive providers in the direction that you intend. Success criteria may vary between tier-one providers depending on the product/service contracted as they are flowed down through the supply chain.
- **Look from the provider's perspective:** Try to see your incentives from the provider's perspective and review what the incentive would make you do in their position. If you choose not to use incentives, consider the behaviours that this may encourage. Considerations may include:
  - Flow down of terms and conditions.
  - Flow down of behaviours.
  - Intellectual property rights management.

The assignment of liabilities for defective work or performance and the ongoing protection of intellectual property rights need to be covered, so that the employer is not tied in to the provider for eternity.

Many of the considerations are generic to almost any package, but how they are implemented may be different dependent upon your perspective. With this in mind, it is useful to put yourself metaphorically in the shoes of your opposite number, particularly when setting/agreeing targets as this will help you to estimate the response of the respondent and for you to gauge whether their corresponding actions will be as you would hope.

In many cases the personnel involved (for the employer and the provider) following handover will be different from those having been responsible for delivery of the solution. This stage therefore will need to include a thorough review by the receiving 'operational' team and a sign-off by their authorised representative that they accept the solution as delivered.

In *service* contracts, such as IT outsourcing arrangements or private finance initiatives (e.g. a toll road), the service or asset is operated by the provider. In this case, in addition to the above mentioned aspects, de-commissioning or handing-back following the defined operating period needs to be covered including circumstances in which this may be done early or late. For example, early hand-back could be due to the provider defaulting on the terms of the contract (resulting in termination), or be due to a changing environment (e.g. the service is just not needed any more).

The key point is that this needs to be thought through, written down and incorporated as part of the contract terms and requirement *before* the contract is entered into.

8.2 Inputs

The inputs to the contract closure, handover, operation and support stage are the outputs from the manage and deliver the contract stage (see section 7.4). The way that these inputs are used will depend on the type of contract.

In the case of a works contract the delivered solution will normally be formed of tangible deliverables that will be operated by the employer under the controlled conditions defined in the 'go-live' information (configuration information, back-up procedures, etc.) and any documentation required for ongoing operations (including any user and installation manuals). The ongoing provider liabilities will consist of any agreed performance guarantees or warranty arrangements or the correction of defective work or materials should they emerge within a set time period following handover.

For *service* contracts, ongoing provider liabilities will be extended to cover the operational duties of the provider that apply once the solution has been delivered. Further inputs will apply consisting of the set of conditions covering satisfactory operation (the performance metrics) and the methods to be employed for measurement and validation against them. In this case ongoing dialogue is implied between the employer and the provider(s), therefore a defined management structure (covering governance and communications) will be necessary. De-commissioning and hand-back following the defined operating period needs to be covered including circumstances in which this may be done early or late.

8.3 Activities

The process is illustrated in Figure 8.1. The activities are segmented into the three major stages:

Contract closure, handover, operation and support

- contract closure (see section 8.5);
- handover (see section 8.6); and
- ongoing operations, maintenance and support (see section 8.7).

These activities follow-on from the decision to close the contract (see section 7.3.7). The 'contract closure' and the 'handover' stages may be conducted in parallel; feeding into the preparation for the 'operation and support' activities.

8.4 Activity 1: Assign resources

The resources that you need to achieve the right conditions to close a contract and to achieve handover are likely to be different from those during delivery; for example increased financial activity may be required. It is beneficial to estimate as soon as practicable the resources that will be required and what must be in place to support the collation of the information needed for efficient use of those resources. Similarly, if it is known during the manage and deliver the contract stage (see Chapter 7) what financial information is going to be required to close the contract, including its format, then this allows gathering of the

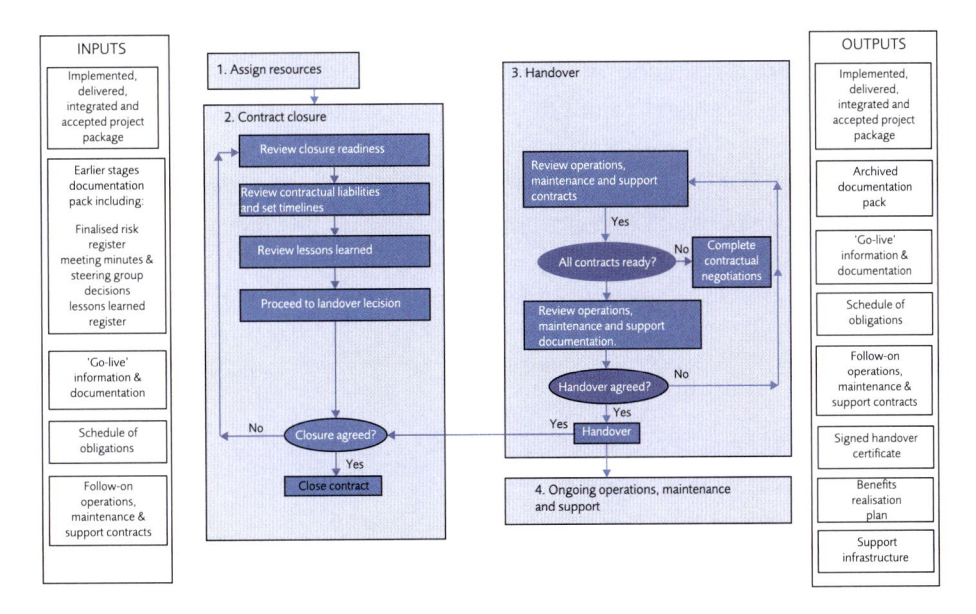

Figure 8.1 Contract closure, handover, operation and support process

APM Guide to Contracts and Procurement

information progressively. This can significantly shorten the closure stage and has the benefit of reducing risk.

Resources are required for the following activities:

- Project closure tasks such as team disbanding and information archiving.
- Financial tasks such as final invoice calculation/compilation and auditing.
- Legal tasks such as any final variation settlements or dispute resolution.
- Operational resources to review and approve handover to the operation stage.
- Technical resource to answer technical questions arising and to conduct training where necessary.
- Management resource to manage the process itself.

It should be noted that the above resources may need to be provided either by the employer or the provider(s) and this responsibility needs to be documented.

8.5 Activity 2: Contract closure

8.5.1 Review closure readiness

As the work associated with the package progresses (see section 7.3.3) the specifics relating to closure (what needs to be done to close it out) should be thought about in preparation.

Following the decision to close the contract (see section 7.3.6) it is necessary to review readiness (i.e. what remains to be done to achieve contract closure and handover). This may be minimal for small and uncomplicated packages but may be significant; dependent on size and complexity (for example where multiple interacting providers are involved).

A *closure readiness review meeting* of the parties involved should be held as soon as practicable after the closure decision. The agenda for this meeting should cover:

1. Overview of the overall project particularly focussing on the project package under consideration for closure.
2. Review of the existing acceptance documentation:
   a. Acceptance criteria have been met/proving trials successfully completed.
   b. Snags have been cleared.
3. Review of the existing operational, maintenance and support documentation.

Contract closure, handover, operation and support

4. Check that archiving has been implemented appropriately with the required retention period.
5. Review of the warranty provisions and any ongoing liabilities of the employer and the provider(s).
6. Review of the key dates identified (contract closure, handover, operation and support timelines see section 8.5.2).
7. Identify follow-on actions; assigning a RACI for each action plus forecast completion date.
8. Set the date for a follow-on review meeting, if needed.

Completion of the contract will be authorised by the employer organisation via a completion certificate or a formal communication to this effect. In the case of input-based contracts, the provider must provide an accurate figure for the cost of all works up to completion (documented in its final invoice) prior to this being submitted. Retention amounts will be in accordance with the contract. It must be ensured that all pertinent materials are accounted for and ownership is transferred formally (per the contract).

At this point it is normal for loaned equipment to be returned or stored for a defined period before destruction and these provisions need to be agreed with the provider including all associated costs before contract completion.

Operational, maintenance and support documentation (as defined in the requirement) must be made available as a deliverable.

8.5.2 Review contractual liabilities and set timelines

Closure of the contract may not discharge all liabilities of the parties. The approach to liabilities should be clearly stated up-front in the contract, including any retention and the conditions under which the liabilities no longer apply.

Examples of ongoing liabilities that can apply for works contracts are:

- Potential legal action (where deadlines have not expired, e.g. fraudulent misrepresentation, procurement irregularities).
- Consequential impacts, e.g. asbestosis liability.
- TUPE liabilities.

Such liabilities are usually handled by the affected parties putting in place a provision, insurance or bond to cover the associated risk (e.g. employer's liability insurance).

Other liabilities for works contracts may be options for contract extension, warranties, parent company guarantees and performance bonds that have a defined timeline. Note that warranties include 'implicit' or 'implied' warranties under general contract law (such as fitness for purpose and merchantable quality) and 'explicit' warranties that are detailed within the specific contract.

In many cases works contracts can be closed following delivery and acceptance of the requirement and successful handover. The ongoing liabilities are often borne by means of financial provisions or insurance as part of the 'normal business' cover of the employer.

Services contracts may well include an operational phase, which brings further liabilities with due timelines covering the operation term and additional follow-on liabilities. For an operational contract there may be a number of key parameters, e.g.

i. Completion of useful life.
ii. Completion of decommissioning.
iii. Date for re-tendering the operational contract.

All of the applying liabilities need to be identified and appropriate cover put in place before the contract is closed.

8.5.3 Review lessons learnt

In the manage and deliver the contract stage we recommended that a *lessons learnt log* be set up as a living document to be updated during delivery.

It is worthwhile to conduct a lessons learnt review activity at the completion point of the overall project, prior to the handover point. The employer organisation's lessons learnt log should be provided to its internal project delivery teams. Lessons learnt activities are almost always worth far more than their cost and can give insights to the follow-on project teams that can save potentially large amounts by the avoidance of common errors.

8.5.4 Proceed to handover decision

The decision to proceed to handover is to be taken by the employer based on the results of activities 8.5.1–8.5.3. If all is in order, then the handover activities can be commenced. It may be appropriate to close the contract at this point or that action may be withheld until after a successful handover, dependent on the risk

Contract closure, handover, operation and support

of flow-back actions that will still need to be taken under the contract. The contract closure panel will need to take a view on the level of risk and close the contract if it is considered to be a low enough risk. Alternatively, the contract may be held open in suspense until handover has been achieved. In many cases handover will not be fully effected until the ultimate capability is up and running successfully (see the example below).

> **Handover example: power station**
>
> Let's take the example of a process job, say a power station: individual components will often be tested at a factory and the employer will want certificates which demonstrate this; they will then be tested to make sure that they fit together (several components are fitted together and a sub-system system tested on-site, e.g. a pressure test). There will then be a commissioning phase where parts of the system are checked to make sure that, in isolation, they work. These parts are progressively added together until the whole system functions. There will then be an optimisation and/or ramping up phase where performance is ramped up and it is optimised to work in accordance with the performance spec requirement. With a power station you don't suddenly run it on full power! Equally, you might be tweaking feedback loops, etc. There might then be a continuous running phase where it has to run to the performance spec requirements for a specified period. In that continuous running phase, the employer's staff might remain involved (perhaps taking some of the benefit if they are generating power and conducting training).
>
> *From this example we see that the exact point of handover may be significantly later than the delivery of the hard asset.*

8.6 Activity 3: Handover

8.6.1 Overview

Handover is the point at which the management and responsibility for the contract deliverables transfers from the provider to the employer organisation or other parties responsible for the ongoing operation and support of the project package. The required ongoing operational and support contracts need to be negotiated and agreed during the preceding manage and deliver the contract stage (see Chapter 7) in order that handover can be achieved without delay following delivery contract closure.

In many cases handover activities are similar to and can be merged with contract closure activities, the exception being the actual award of the ongoing operational and support contracts (unless the delivery contract includes providing operation and support).

For large or complex project packages, it may be a lower risk for both the employer and the provider to stage the handover. This approach gives confidence that achieving final handover will be on-schedule; or alternatively prompts an action plan for recovery. Handover stages may include, for example:

- Testing.
- Commissioning.
- Staged handover of deliverables.

A successful handover requires, in addition to a delivered and operation-ready requirement, the outputs from the above contract closure activities such as:

- An information package (e.g. as designed/as built).
- Training manuals.
- Trained operators.
- Operations and maintenance manuals.
- Asset integration data.
- A recommended spares holding and maintenance-led spares ordering triggers.
- Shared learning from the project delivery (lessons learnt).

8.7 Activity 4: Ongoing operation, maintenance and support activities

Ongoing operation, maintenance and support activities can range from the basic honouring of warranty provisions through to the management of a follow-on *service contract*.

The ongoing owner of the business benefits will judge whether the business benefits being delivered remain worthwhile. Attention needs to be paid to continuity, although the ongoing owner will not necessarily be the same person as the package-delivery sponsor.

In most cases operations, maintenance and support will be handled by means of a new contractual arrangement covering all activities beyond handover.

During the *support* stage a whole life view of the asset or service needs to be taken including the element of *challenging whether the benefit is provided* – is there still a business need or have priorities/circumstances changed?

The focus will be on delivery of business benefits as set out in the full business case (FBC) (see Chapter 2), i.e. the basis for justifying the original investment. The FBC should have set out the requirement for post-delivery review to assess delivery of benefits (reviews being repeated at appropriate points over the life of the support contract). Reviews should check that:

- The expected benefits are being delivered (regular reporting of performance and improvement opportunities).
- The relationship with operations and support providers plus the potential to improve are being actively managed.

A *benefits realisation plan* (see section 2.3.1) can be a useful aid; providing guidance on how to:

- Manage performance.
- Maintain/improve on performance.
- Manage change to scope and operation during operation.

The main considerations for smooth running of operational services are:

1. Requirements definition and stakeholder issues.
2. Developing the operational services contract:
    a. Clear ownership of requirements and outcomes from the service.
    b. Senior management and other key stakeholders are fully committed.
    c. Thorough attention to risk management by all involved in delivery.
    d. Shared understanding across the delivery chain of how the service will be provided.
    e. Appropriate measures for performance, quality and budgets.
3. Managing the operational services contract:
    a. Adequate skills and resources provided by all parties to the contract – throughout the life of the contract.
    b. Continual checking and revisiting of key assumptions.

c. Ensuring context, complexities and interdependencies of the contract are well understood by everyone involved.
   d. Excellent governance arrangements.
4. Looking to the future:
   a. Formal change control procedures that everyone follows.
   b. Appropriate incentives for continuous improvement.
   c. Potential changes ahead considered and planned for, linked to ongoing business strategy.
   d. Future supplier arrangements considered, such as exit strategy and re-competition.

8.8 Outputs

The outputs from the contract closure, handover, operation and support stage will vary depending on the nature of the required ongoing activities. The main outputs are likely to be:

- 'Go-live' information (configuration information, back-up procedures, etc.).
- The documentation required for ongoing operations (including any user and installation manuals).
- A schedule of obligations that need to be fulfilled during ongoing operations, such as performance metrics and criteria that may be linked to a performance guarantee and against which funds are withheld.
- Follow-on provider contracts that will be commenced following handover. These contracts will have been negotiated during the earlier stages in the overall procurement cycle.
- A support infrastructure, which could include helpdesk resources, technical support personnel (e.g. on-call), service level agreement (SLA) metrics and review, management resources, offices and IT facilities, asset register, spares holding (potentially held at multiple geographical locations) and resources to undertake obsolescence management.
- A *benefits realisation plan*, where appropriate, to detail the assessment criteria for the ongoing benefits being provided. This will also form an input to the decision to terminate ongoing operations (e.g. due to obsolescence or economic factors).

Acronyms and abbreviations

APM	Association for Project Management
BCS	British Computer Society
BOOT	Build, own, operate, transfer
BOT	Build, operate, transfer
CIPS	Chartered Institute of Procurement and Supply
CRC	Cooperative Research Centres (Australia)
CV	Curriculum vitae
DBFO	Design, build, finance, operate
ECI	Early contractor involvement
EU	European Union
FBC	Full business case
GMP	Guaranteed maximum price
HR	Human resources
IPR	Intellectual property rights
IRR	Internal rate of return
ISO	International Standards Organisation
IT	Information technology
ITT	Invitation to tender
JV	Joint venture
KO	Kick-off (meeting)
MEAT	Most economically advantageous tender
NDA	Non-disclosure agreement
NEC3	New Engineering Contract version 3
NRM	New rules of measurement
MOD	Ministry of Defence
MRP	Material requirements planning
OGC	Office of Government Commerce
PaBS	Package breakdown structure
PESTLE	Political, economic, sociological, technological, legal, environmental
PFI	Private finance initiative

Acronyms and abbreviations

P3 (PPP)	Project, programme and portfolio or Public, Private Partnership
PQQ	Preliminary qualification questionnaire
PSP	Provider selection panel
RACI	Responsible, accountable, consulted, informed
RFI	Request for information
RIBA	Royal Institute of British Architects
ROI	Return on investment
SBC	Strategic business case
SLA	Service level agreement
SME	Subject matter expert
SoW	Statement of work
SPV	Special purpose vehicle
SWOT	Strengths, weaknesses, opportunities, threats
TA	Technical authority
ToR	Terms of reference
TUPE	Transfer of Undertakings (Protection of Employment)
UK	United Kingdom
VAT	Value added tax
WBS	Work breakdown structure

Bibliography

Act of Parliament. (2002). *Enterprise Act 2002*. London: HM Stationery Office.

APM. (n.d.). *APM Body of Knowledge 6th edition*. APM.

Bakshi, A. (1995). Alliances Change Economics of Andrew Field Development. *Offshore Engineer*, 50(1).

Bensaou, M. (1999). Portfolios of Buyer–Supplier Relationships. *Sloan Management Review*, 15 July.

Broome, J. (2002). *Procurement Routes for Partnering: A Practical Guide*. London: ICE Publishing.

Broome, J. (2016). Point of Law. *Project*, 56–58.

Chartered Institute of Procurement and Supply (CIPS). (n.d.). Retrieved from CIPS: www.cips.org.

CIPS. (2014). *Supplier Incentivisation*. Retrieved from www.cips.org: www.cips.org/Documents/Knowledge/Procurement-Topics-and-Skills/10-Developing-and-Managing-Contracts/Contract-Management/Supplier_Incentivisation.pdf.

Deming, W. E. (1986). *Out of the Crisis*. Cambridge, MA: MIT Press.

Dhanushkodi, U. (2012). *Contract Strategy for Construction Projects*. Manchester: University of Manchester Faculty of Engineering and Physical Sciences.

Encyclopaedia Britannica. (2010). Retrieved from www.britannica.com: www.britannica.com/event/Deepwater-Horizon-oil-spill-of-2010.

European Union. (1993). *Guide to the Community Rules on Public Works Contracts (Directive 93/37/EEC)*. European Union.

Fenn, P. and Gameson, R. (1992). Construction Conflict Management and Resolution. *Proceedings of the First International Construction Management Conference*. Manchester, UK: E. & F.N. Spon.

Ganes, A. and Naevdal, S. (2008). *Software Contracting and Agile Development in the Norwegian ICT Industry – A Qualitative Survey*. NTNU.

IACCM. (2011). *The Operational Guide – Contract and Commercial Management*. London: Van Haren Publishing.

IACCM. (2013). *Fundamentals of Contract and Commercial Management*. London: Van Haren Publishing.

Kajewski, S. (2006). *Guidelines for Successful eTendering Implementation*. Brisbane: Cooperative Research Centre (CRC) for Construction Innovation.

Bibliography

Kraljic, P. (1983). Purchasing Must Become Supply Management. *Harvard Business Review*.

NEC. (2015). *Early Contractor Involvement (ECI)*. London: NEC.

Newberry, T. and Watkins, P. (2012). *APM C&P SIG Masterclass 5 – Selecting the Right Provider*. Retrieved from www.apm.org.uk: www.apm.org.uk/sites/default/files/open/CP%20Masterclass%205%20Selecting%20the%20Right%20Provider%20Rev.pdf.

Nijssen, J. (2015). *When Contract Management Meets PRINCE2*. Kampen, the Netherlands: Pinetop BV.

OGC. (n.d.). *Gateway Process* publications. OGC.

Porter, M. E. (2008). The Five Competitive Forces That Shape Strategy. *Harvard Business Review*.

Revay, S. G. (1993). Can Construction Claims Be Avoided? *Building Research and Information*, 21(1), 56–58.

RIBA. (2013). *RIBA Plan of Work 2013*. RIBA.

RICS. (2013). *New Rules of Measurement*. RICS.

RICS. (2014). *Appropriate Contract Selection*. RICS.

Rocque, B. L. (n.d.). *PMP, Enabling Effective Project Sponsorship: A Coaching Framework for Starting Projects Well*. Retrieved from http://threehousesconsulting.com/docs/RocqueProceeding.pdf.

Soames, B. (2011). *Buying Just Like The Ancient Greeks: What Ancient Greek Purchasing Can Teach Us About Procurement Now*. Buy Research Publications.

Tate, M. (2015). *A Practitioner's Guide to Selection and Procurement*. BCS The Chartered Institute for IT.

UK Act of Parliament. (1998). *Competition Act 1998*. London: HM Stationery Office.

UK Crown Commercial Service. (2016). *A Brief Guide to the 2014 EU Public Procurement Directives*. London: UK Crown Commercial Service.

UK Ministry of Defence. (2013). *Better Defence Acquisition*. The Stationery Office.

Ward, G. (2008). *The Project Manager's Guide to Purchasing – Contracting for Goods and Services*. London: Gower Publishing Ltd.

www.gov.uk. (2014, October). *Early Contractor Involvement*. Retrieved from www.gov.uk: www.gov.uk/government/uploads/system/uploads/attachment_data/file/377586/Early_contractor_involvement__ECI__guidance__Oct_2014_.pdf.

Yates, A. (1991) 'Procurement and construction management' in P. Venmore-Rowland, P. Brandon and T. Mole (eds), *Investment, Procurement and Performance in Construction*, London: E. & F. N. Spon.

Appendix A – Generic procurement and contracting risks

Table A1 provides examples of the typical risks that are associated with external contracting together with containment/preventative measures and contingencies that may be applicable and that should be accounted for during the selection process.

Table A1 Typical risks associated with external contracting

Risk description	Possible containment/preventative measures
First time use of a provider – performance may be unsatisfactory (cost, time, quality).	• Prior research of a provider's track record (reference customers, published, performance measures, case studies, working practices). • Generate a detailed statement of work (SoW) that clearly states objectives and performance measures and ensure this is referenced in the contract. • Payment milestones linked to specific gates, deliverables and performance measures with contract termination as an option. • Ensure that the provider generates a full proposal, cross-referenced to the SoW, including a plan for the contracted works with milestones identifying deliverables, an identified project manager and issue escalation process. • Allocate responsibility for provider management (usually the overall project manager) and ensure close monitoring of progress and performance including face-to-face meetings and access to working resources for quality/working practice assessment. • Mandate the generation of a quality plan by the provider, requiring approval by the employer. • Mandate the generation of a risk management plan by the provider detailing containment measures and contingencies.
The provider may leave the consortium – bankruptcy, change of management, loss of personnel resources.	• Prior research of the provider's solvency. • Ensure that the contract includes provision for the termination by the provider with appropriate compensation measures. • Close communications (often prior-notice of problems may be evident from general communications, unavailability of resources, etc.)

Incompatible working practices (Differences in process, terminology and culture) – errors and inefficiency may be introduced due to differences in terminology/language, processes, organisational structures and local cultures. Once the contract is in place and work has commenced if misunderstandings develop then additional management time will be required to investigate and determine the 'delta' in understanding.

- Ensure that the SoW requires the provider to supply a description of its standard procedures and how these will be employed to undertake the contract works.
- Detail the reporting requirements in the SoW.
- Obtain a copy of the provider's procedures manual or methodology at bid-time.
- Obtain an organisational chart for the contracted resources to be employed in the project with channels for escalation.
- Agree on a language that will be used throughout the project at bid-time (English). Agree on formats for date and time
- Ensure that the project kick-off meeting includes a review of working practice alignment and have available templates for key deliverable documents.
- Ensure that sufficient provision for progress meetings is made. Supply a performa agenda for meetings.
- It will help greatly if the employer's project manager makes a positive effort to understand any challenges from the provider's perspective as often misunderstandings are just as problematic for the provider and mitigation is likely to be a joint initiative.

Poor progress/financial reporting – the provider may not give sufficient information to allow progress between milestones to be gauged or cost-to-complete to be gauged in input-based contracts.

- Clearly state the reporting requirements in the SoW and ensure that these are acknowledged in the provider's proposal document.
- Introduce mandatory reporting in the pricing document as a condition of prompt payment.
- In input-based contracts mandate the inclusion of estimate to complete in regular progress reports and ensure that these are phased appropriately with the main project reporting schedule (ensure that invoicing is also appropriately phased for cash flow management).

(Continued)

Table A1 Continued

Risk description	Possible containment/preventative measures
Poor change control – the provider may initiate uncontrolled changes (e.g. add/remove functionality through ad-hoc communications).	• The SoW should include a change control procedure and this should be referenced in the contract document, including provision that the employer must approve the change prior to it taking place. • Ensure that approval authority for changes is assigned by both parties.
Poaching of work or personnel – providers may campaign to work directly with the employer, or recruit key personnel.	• Ensure that the contract includes an appropriate clause to prevent solicitation of work or recruitment of personnel by the provider. • Ensure that all contractual communications are channelled through appropriate channels. • Where the provider is a known competitor restrict access appropriately. Don't include them on the tender list unless there is a good reason to do so. • Be aware of the dangers and escalate to your commercial manager should any contravention be suspected. • Agree the approach with the employer and get them to attend meetings to show their support for you as the employer's project manager.
Export control issues – where export licences are required work/communications may be delayed until all licences are granted.	• Where the provider also requires putting in place an export licence ensure applications are coordinated. • Ensure that all export-related communications carry the appropriate export licence statement. • Use clear terms in the contract.
IPR issues – there may be misunderstanding of the ownership of intellectual property rights (IPR).	• Be realistic about what IP the parties can actually claim/own. • Determine the ownership of IPR at the bid phase and include a clear statement in the SoW detailing ownership. • Ensure that project personnel are aware of the IPR provisions for the project.

Conflicts in division of work – providers may duplicate work being done by others.

- Clearly state the ownership of work packages in the SoW and ensure that this is acknowledged in the provider's proposal document.
- Consider a scope responsibility matrix to define who is doing what.
- Spend time on managing the various interfaces across the programme.
- Ensure that the provider's project plan is in alignment with the employer's project plan.

Poor support provision – providers may not provide the appropriate level of support for related tasks in the project or for post-delivery support.

- Ensure that the SoW states clearly the level of support required.
- Include a resource histogram in the bid and contract documents.

Award of contract (AOC) slippage – the employer's overall contract may take longer than expected to be signed and this will result in a corresponding delay in the signing of provider contracts, which are negotiated during the stage of contract finalisation.

There is a risk that the employer may sign-up to fixed delivery dates that are no longer in-line with the 'AOC + N weeks' dates in the provider contract(s) leading to potentially another negotiation round with the selected provider(s).

- Request an instruction to proceed (ITP) with limit of liability (LoL) from the employer to allow initial works to proceed.
- Build a risk-buffer into milestones in anticipation of slippage in signing of the overall contract.
- Allow in the employer's risk budget for increased resources to be applied to catch-up and include flowed-up costs from the providers (e.g. overtime working).
- Proceed at risk prior to contract signing: This is not a recommended strategy except in specific cases where there are extenuating circumstances (e.g. other related contracts may be adversely affected). This decision would need to be taken by the employer's senior executive management.

(Continued)

Table A1 Continued

Risk description	Possible containment/preventative measures
Re-assignment of risk (uncontrolled risk transference) – in meetings during delivery a provider may allude to a risk having been transferred to the employer from the provider. The risk of this occurring increases with the number of providers and also if the related SoWs may not have been sufficiently clear or specific.	• Enforce a strict change control procedure, which should, ideally, be described in all SoWs. • Ensure that all meetings are minuted. • Add a disclaimer to minutes performa such as: 'These minutes do not constitute approval of any change to the contract or reassignment of risk and any proposed change will be subject to the agreed change control procedure.' • Ensure that meeting minutes are subject to review. • Include review of the risk register in progress reviews.
Dependency linkages – where there are several tiers of provider dependencies need to flow upwards appropriately. A second tier provider's dependency may actually be linked to the employer's works, but not properly acknowledged in the respective contract.	• At bid time make the need to define all dependencies a priority for the employer and all providers. • Be wary of accepting a proposal that has little or no dependencies or risks defined. • Include clear dependency linkages in the schedule and examine these at each progress review.
Acceptance ambiguity – the employer's authority may accept the provider's deliverable (e.g. a sub-system) in isolation without proper integration and then find integration issues that require diagnosis and corrective action from the provider.	• Hold a significant retention that is only releasable at full system sign-off. • Test and verification plans are typically developed during the planning phase. • Guard against test and verification plans that specify isolated tests of sub-systems. If isolated tests are necessary then implement a phased sign-off based on initial and final (integrated) tests.
Review cycle delays – documents authored during the planning and implementation phases often require inputs from all parties and are therefore subject to reviews to ensure that all have 'bought-in' to the final approved version. Often, provision is not made for the time that is taken for reviews and therefore work may be delayed until all parties agree and sign off documents.	• Define efficient mechanisms for secure transfer of documents between all parties. • Schedule specific review gateways and meetings. • Consider co-location of parties at key decision points. • Define time limits for review. • Create and circulate a full documentation plan with (responsible, accountable, consulted and informed) matrix that identifies ownership of priority documents.

- **Requirement creep** – an employer's team member instructs a lower tier provider directly resulting in unbudgeted work that is unexpectedly billed to a higher tier provider.

- **Diminishing resource priority** – there is a risk that the personnel assigned to delivery may be less qualified and inexperienced than those assigned at the bid phase, thus causing work to be of a lower quality or protracted.

- **Single source dependency** – single-source providers may be difficult to control as they are effectively bottleneck. Poor performance of a single-source provider is a relatively high risk and will need to be very carefully monitored if a single source is the only solution.

  Undertaking a formal selection process can supply a clear understanding why there is a single source as this can feed into containment actions.

- The key to ensuring that requirements do not 'creep' as a result of direct communications is to mandate that all of such communications are documented and copied to the employer.
- The early exercising of the change control procedure by the employer, even for a 'nil impact' technical change will often focus the parties on adherence to the proper formalities and avoid drifting into creep of requirements.

- Specific named personnel may be specified in the contract or SoW (albeit this might be in very specialised 'consultancy' type roles) however it is not always possible for named personnel to be available.
- SoWs should state that provider personnel should "hold appropriate qualifications and be sufficiently experienced". Ideally outline CVs of the provider's proposed personnel should be requested in order that any replacements can be assessed like-for-like.
- The possibility of change or loss of personnel should be included in the employer and provider risk registers with appropriate containment and mitigation proposals.
- Employer project managers should actively assess the capability of provider personnel during the planning and implementation phases.

- Always have a 'plan B' to replace the single-source even though this may be unpalatably costly (accordingly include in the risk register).
- Make sure that the single source knows there is an alternative.
- Identify a clear payment milestone plan with gating and break clauses.
- Act on any flowed-up dependencies as a priority.
- Monitor the single source intensively for prior warning of issues (consider co-locating personnel for day-to-day monitoring).
- Record in detail any underperformance.

(*Continued*)

Table A1 Continued

Risk description	Possible containment/preventative measures
Insufficient levels of authority – the provider's personnel managing the project may not have a sufficient level of authority to make the necessary key decisions thus causing delays due to the provider's governance process.	• At bid-time, request the names, positions and contact details of the provider's key personnel who may be called upon to resolve issues for example; senior executive, divisional executives (where several divisions are involved), quality manager and these personnel should be included in the employer's stakeholder management plan. • Agree an escalation route for issues. • Carefully document any risks and issues (e.g. events leading up to the problem) for consideration by the provider's senior management.

Appendix B – Example tender report template

TENDER REPORT

Project number ....
Project title ....
Project manager ....
Location ....
Discipline ....

Title	**Name**	**Signature**	**Date**
Director of estates projects	....	....	....
Senior supplier	....	....	....
Category manager (Construction)	....	....	....
Project manager	....	....	....
Cost manager	....	....	....

Contents

1. Executive summary
2. Introduction
3. Tender process
4. Tenders received
5. Detailed tender analysis
6. Tender interviews
7. Programme
8. Value engineering options
9. Further potential savings
10. Conclusion and recommendations

Typical appendices:
Appendix A – Tender returns inc. form of tender
Appendix B – Detailed tender comparison

Appendix B – Example tender report template

Appendix C – Post tender interview scoring
Appendix D – Post tender queries/correspondence

1. Executive summary

Description of works
Describe the works that are programmed to be completed including any abnormal items. [No more than two A4 pages]

Tender values

Original Budget	
Approved Budget	

	Approved Budget	Tenderer 1	Tenderer 2	Tenderer 3	Tenderer 4
Preliminaries					
Building Work					
M&E Work					
External Works					
Overheads & Profit					
Construction Cost	**£0**	**£0**	**£0**	**£0**	**£0**
Project Risk					
Design Fees					
College Direct Contracts					
VAT					
Project Cost	**£0**	**£0**	**£0**	**£0**	**£0**
Value Engineering					
Potential Savings					

Expand the above table as necessary to suit specifics of tender.
[Double Click on table to edit]

Reasons for variance
Explain the reason why there is a variance between the original budget and the approved budget and then the tendered figure.

Potential value engineering options
Detail any steps that are possible to reduce/increase this variance if applicable.

Recommendations
Please state your recommended supplier with reasons.

Next Steps
Please advise what the next steps are in order to commence this project.

Appendix B – Example tender report template

2. Introduction

Project overview.

3. Tender process

Please detail the tender process; including evaluation criteria.

4. Tenders received

Please list the names of the tenders received.

5. Detailed tender analysis

Please insert your excel spreadsheet comparison; Include normalisation of tender returns.

6. Tender interviews

Please document information gathered from pre/mid and post tender interviews.

7. Programme

Please provide a commentary on any programme related issues included in the tenders received.

8. Value engineering options

Please explain any value engineering and cost saving measures there are and then potential savings that could be made.

9. Further potential savings

Please detail any further potential savings that could be made that require further discussion.

10. Conclusion and recommendations

Please detail your conclusions and recommendations for the tender.

Appendix C – Red flags

Table C1 Red flags

Topic	Red flag
Bribery and corruption	Award of subsidiary contracts in advance of the main contract.
	Retaining, regaining or obtaining works
	Abuse of position (use of insider information, gifts and hospitality)
	Misrepresentation (tailoring documents, altering submissions, charging for unused work/materials)
	Failing to disclose (inaccurate information, differing information to each bidder)
	Ignoring process consistently
	Forcing through orders
	Continuing to use a poor supplier
	Anger when challenged
	Winning all the work
	Regular 'emergency' work
Concealing conflicts of interest	Related share interests
	1 on 1 meetings with suppliers
	Negative returns of a COI form when it is blatant
	Winning bidder drafts the spec
	Regular offsite meetings with no expenses claimed
	Moving job to a provider – risk of insider information
Manipulation of the specification	Specification narrowness – favouring a particular provider
	Low number of bids received
	Evaluation process not followed
	Unauthorised sign-off
	Specification narrowness

(*Continued*)

Appendix C – Red flags

Table C1 *Continued*

Topic	Red flag
Bid rigging	Same companies win/lose repeatedly
	Main competitors not bidding
	Suppliers seemingly taking it in turns to bid lowest
	Low number of bids received
	Inconsistent bid rates from bid to bid
	Bid rates suddenly lower when a new supplier is introduced
	Same suppliers listed to bid on lots of different commodities
	Very 'similar' RFP submissions
	Unlikely bid winners
	Submission of significantly higher price
	Provider deliberately not compliant with tender instructions
	Provider deliberately does not meet specification
Ghost companies	Holding companies that don't trade
	Provider whose name sounds like a major player, but isn't
	Provider's logo does not match the services offered
	Company structure is not transparent
	Local company registered overseas.
	Company generally unknown in the applicable market
	Can't provide references
	Recently formed company
	Invoice values are round amounts
	Bank account details on invoices don't match registration details or A/P details

Appendix C – Red flags

Sole source	Service could easily have been tendered but wasn't
	No market price checking undertaken
	Commodity not previously sole sourced
	No justification of sole source
	Poor reasoning for provider selection
	New type of work for this provider, or not their core business
	Same provider but now at a higher cost
	Regular gifts or hospitality

Index

Figures and tables are in *italics*. Definitions are in **bold**

adjudication, and disputes 86–7
affordability criteria 20
agendas 148
'agile' project delivery 10–11
alliances 72–4
amendments 78
arbitration 87
archives, document 31
award of contracts 140

benefit, definition of 20
benefits realisation plan 20, 171
Bensaou model 47, 49
'best fit' contracting strategy 62–77, *64*, 87–9
'best value' principle 114–15, 124–5, *126*
bi-party contract 56
bonds, guarantee 83
BOOT (build, own, operate, transfer) contracts 75
BOT (build, operate, transfer) contracts 75
bottleneck items *48*
boundaries *46*, 89
breaches, of contract 78
budgets, outline 35, 62–3
build, operate, transfer (BOT) contracts 75
build, own, operate, transfer (BOOT) contracts 75
business case, definition of 19
business case sponsor 20–1
buyer–supplier relationships, definition of *50*

captive buyers, definition of *50*
captive suppliers, definition of *50*
change control process 144–5, *144*, 154–6, *154*

clarifications, final 137
closure, definition of 161
closure strategy 163, 165–6
collateral warranties 83–4
communications 118, 149
completion, of contract 156
complex projects 44
concept and feasibility 15–31, *18*
confidentiality 118–19
constraints 60, 89, 107–8
construction industry 54, 92
consultations 149–50
contract closure *157*, 158, 162–3, 166–9
contract closure, definition of 161
contract, definition of 13
contracting strategy, packaging 2, 53–89, *59*, *62–77*, 144
Contracts (Rights of Third Parties) Act (1999) 84
cost
    influence curve *9*
    reimbursable contracts 68–9
    savings 54
    target 70–1, *71*, 81
cost influence curve *9*
criteria
    affordability 20
    final selection 131–3
    'make or buy' 40–3, *41–3*
    scoring, providers and 128–30, *132*, 135, *136*
    success 158, 163
custom and practice, foreign countries and 100

damages, liquidated 79–80

193

Index

DBFO (design, build, finance and operate) contracts 75–6, 77
definition phase, planning and 149–50
delivery
    'agile' project 10–11
    manage and 141–59
    options 26
    solution 142–3, *143*
delivery options 26
Deming circle 151
design, build, finance and operate (DBFO) contracts 75–6, 77
developing requirements 105–7
dispute resolution processes 84–7
documents
    archives 31
    briefing 89, 95, 100–3, 122
    contractual 137–9, 142–3
drafting contracts 103, 104–5, 142
driving factors, contract 59–60

employer, definition of 12
engineering industry 92
EQQ (extended qualification questionnaire) 131
EU (European Union) legislation 38
extended qualification questionnaire (EQQ) 131

FBC ('full' business case) 16, 30–1, 95
feasibility, concept and 15–31, *18*
fee based arrangements: 68
final selection criteria 131–3
'Five Forces Analysis' 47
foreign countries, law of 99–100
'full' business case (FBC) 16, 30–1, 95

gate reviews 18, 28
gate reviews, definition of 28
GMP (guaranteed maximum price) contract 71, *71*
goods, definition of 13
governance 29, 30
governance, definition of 29
governing law 95–100
government contracts 40, 60

guaranteed maximum price (GMP) 71, *71*
guarantees, providers and 82–3

handover 168, 169–70
handover, definition of 162
housing associations *126*

implementation cycle 151–3
incentives, use of 79–81, 163
industry sectors 25–6, 35, 54, 92
information gathering 59–61
information sharing 119
initiation process 145, *145*
intellectual property (IP) 118–19, 163
internal rate of return (IRR) 25
international law 99–100
investment, relative 47
invitation to tender (ITT) 132–4, 135
IP (intellectual property) 118–19, 163
IRR (internal rate of return) 25
ITT (invitation to tender) 132–4, 135

joint venture (JV) 74–7
jurisdiction, foreign countries and 99
JV (joint venture) 74–7

key roles 146, 147
key terminology, contracts and 89, 95
KO (kick-off) meeting 147–8
Kraljic matrix 47, *48*, 49, 55

law
    governing 95–100
    international 99–100
    UK 96–9
lead-times, critical 39–40
legal profession 94, 95–100, 139
legal requirements, contract terms and 96–9, 117, 122
lessons learnt 168
leverage (purchasing power) *48*
liability, contractual 55, 80, 157, 163, 164, 167–8
life cycle stages *3*, *6*

194

Index

liquidated damages 79–80
litigation 87

maintenance and support 171–2
'make or buy' criteria 40–3, *41–3*
manage and delivery 141–59
management based contracts 69
market consultations 38
market exchanges, definition of *50*
material requirements planning (MRP) system 149
MEAT (most economically advantageous tender) 114–15
meeting, KO (kick-off) 147–8
methodologies, procurement *127*
most economically advantageous tender (MEAT) 114–15
MRP (material requirements planning) system 149

NDA's (non-disclosure agreements) 119
needs, identified 17
non-critical (standardised products) *48*
non-disclosure agreements (NDA's) 119

operation and support, definition of 162
operations management, definition of 162
operations, ongoing 170–2
outcomes, variation 56

PABS (package breakdown structure) 14, 33–4, 37–9, 43–52, *45*
package breakdown structure (PABS) 14, 33–4, 37–9, 43–52, *45*
package, definition of 13
PESTLE (acronym) 60–1
PFI (private finance initiative) 75, *76*, 77
planning
    benefits realisation 20, 171
    defined 17
    definition phase 149–50
    management 95

MRP (material requirements planning) system 149
plans, defined 17
portfolio management 7
power, purchasing *48*
power station example *38*, 44, 169
PPP (public private partnerships) 76, 77
PQQ (pre-qualification questionnaire) 128–31
pre-qualification questionnaire (PQQ) 128–31
presentations, provider 133–5
private finance initiative (PFI) 75, *76*, 77
problem-solving 93–4
procurement, definition of 12
procurement process 7
programme management 7
project
    'agile' delivery of 10–11
    alliances 72–3
    board 30
    brief 22, 37
    complex 44
    life cycle of *6*
    procurement in context 2–4
    relationships *51*, 58
    risk 54–8
    scope statements 18, 27
    sponsor 29
    wind-farm example *45*
project board (board), definition of 30
project risk (risk), definition of 55
project sponsor (sponsorship), definition of 29
proposals 138, 139
provider, definition of 12–13
provider selection panel (PSP) 122, 123–4, *123*
providers, potential 34–6, 39–40, 59–60, 83, 125
PSP (provider selection panel) 122, 123–4, *123*
public private partnerships (PPP) 76, 77

reality checks, provider 134–5
red flags, legal compliance 117
reimbursable contracts 68–9
relationships, nature of project *51*, 58
requests for information (RFIs) 40

Index

requirement, definition of 13
requirements
    developing 105–7
    hierarchy *5*, *36*
    legal 96–9, 122
    MRP (material requirements planning) system 149
    terms and *38*, *44*, 91–111, *101*, 122, 138
retention payments 81–2
return on investment (ROI) 25
reviews
    contract 107–10, 146
    gate 18, 28
    objective 117
    periodic 93
RFIs (requests for information) 40
risk
    assessments 27
    de-risking 150
    events 54–5, 78–9
    minor 57
    third-party 78–9
    transfer threshold 77–9
risk event, definition of 54
risk management 20, 54–9, 120–1, 144, 153
risk owner, definition of 55
ROI (return on investment) 25
rules of interpretation 108–10

savings, cost 54
SBC ('strategic' business case) 16, 17, 19–20, 27–8, 37
scope, definition of 27
scope statements 37
scoring criteria, providers and 128–30, *132*, *135*, *136*
selection process
    final criteria 131–3
    provider 113–20, *136*
    PSP (provider selection panel) 122, 123–4, *123*
    teams 120
services contracts 163–4, 168
services, definition of 13

solution delivery 142–3, *143*
sourcing, externally 34
sourcing, internally 34
SoW (statement of work) 138–9, 146
sponsors 20–1, 29
stakeholder, definition of 21
stakeholder management, definition of 21
stakeholders, key 18, 20, 21–4, 26
standard conditions 87–8, 102–3
statement of work (SoW) 138–9, 146
strategic alliances 73–4
'strategic' business case (SBC) 16, 17, 19–20, 27–8, 37
strategic items 47, *48*
strategic partnerships, definition of *50*
strategies 17, 33–52, *37*
subject matter experts, definition of 120
success criteria 158, 163
success criteria, definition of 23
support infrastructures 171–2
SWOT matrix *24*, 61

target costs 70–1, *71*, 81
technical proposals 138
termination, of contract 157–8
terminology, key 89, 95
terms and requirements *38*, *44*, 91–111, *101*, 122, 138
tools, operation 149
trends, recent procurement 5–10

UK case law and legislation 96–9
uncertainty, reducing 110

variation outcomes 56

warranties, collateral 83–4
WBS (work breakdown structure) 14
WBS (work breakdown structure), definition of 39
wind-farm project example *45*
work breakdown structure (WBS) 14
works contracts *5*, *36*
works, definition of 14